# NEW ORLEANS DRINKS
# AND
# HOW TO MIX THEM

By

### JACK D. L. HOLMES, Ph.D.*

*Doctor of Pleasure and Happiness

NEW ORLEANS                    MCMLXXIII

HOPE PUBLICATIONS
P.O. Box 10062
New Orleans, Louisiana   70121

# Dedication

For all my drinking friends, then and now, here and there, but especially for Bob and Cathy Coleman who first shared New Orleans drinks with me.

# TABLE OF CONTENTS

*Page*

Introduction ........................................................................... 5

Basic Mixologist Tips ........................................................... 8

Some Historical Highlights on New Orleans Booze ............ 10

Eye-openers and Morning-after Remedies ......................... 18

Absinthe Makes the Heart Grow Fonder? ........................... 21

Sazerac — the Authentic New Orleans Drink .................... 24

Henry Ramos and His Famous Fizz .................................... 27

Southern Comfort — Happy Marriage of Bourbon and Peaches .... 29

Fruit Recipes Betty Crocker Doesn't Know ....................... 31

Sweet Cordial Drinks ............................................................ 33

Reverend Craig's Friendly Potable ..................................... 39

"The Happy Accident" — Brandy or Cognac? .................... 45

"It's Gin, Gin, Gin that Makes you . . ." .......................... 49

Yo, Ho, Ho, Admiral Vernon ............................................... 53

¡Viva México! — Tequila, Pulque and other Cactus Juice ........ 57

Tovarisch — Vodka, Slivovitz, Äkvavit, *et al* ................. 61

Apple Brandy — to Keep the Doctor Away? ...................... 64

A Day Without Wine is Like a Day Without Sunshine ....... 66

Beer — Man's Oldest and Best Friend ............................... 68

Coffee and Antifreeze .......................................................... 70

Thanks, But I'm on the Wagon ............................................ 74

New Orleans Bars .................................................................. 76

Toasts for the Occasion ........................................................ 86

More Reading About Booze .................................................. 88

Index ....................................................................................... 90

# Introduction

The title of this book is somewhat misleading. This *is* about New Orleans drinks and how to mix them, but it is more than that. In one sense the book is a marriage of my own interests: history and drinking. For fifteen years my historical research has taken me to New Orleans and libraries from New York to California, to foreign archives in England, Portugal, France, Spain and Mexico. At the same time, "man shall not live by history alone," as it is written. I have had the good fortune to sample the wines and liquors of various nations and regions. One of the best ways to learn a language and the culture of another land is to bend elbows with the natives.

My memories of my odyssey are as warm and vivid many years later as they were at the time. My first visit to a brewery in Monterrey, where the Cervecería Cuauhtémoc generously provided unlimited cups of cold Carta Blanca beer, started me off. Since that time I have toured breweries in Houston and St. Louis, the fourteenth century brewery of Löewenbrau in Munich, the Heineken brewery in Amsterdam and the Guinness stout producers of old Dublin. The Jackson Brewing Company of New Orleans offers its visitors similar tours.

I can recall with great pleasure sampling the wines of Europe as my research drove me through many countries — packing snow into a glass in the Swiss Alps and pouring *vin ordinaire* over it; the rich blood-like wines of Galicia; the Catalán wines poured from a *porrón;* the *valdapeñas* of central Spain, sampled through the narrow opening of a goat-skin *bota;* the shared wine among newfound friends in Segovia; and the Mardi-gras-like excitement of the 1964 Fiesta de San Fermín in Pamplona. In the United States the only place I have ever felt the same is in New Orleans, and not just at Carnival.

The secret to good drinking is, of course, moderation. "Moderation in all things" is a fine motto. One day while I was having a *copa* or two of the smooth solera sherry in a bodega of Sevilla, nibbling on the delicious shrimp *tapas,* my eyes were directed to a sign behind the bar. This is translated below:

IS THERE ANYTHING BETTER THAN WINE?

"The act of drinking is an art which only the races of ancient lineage possess. When one makes use of wine moderately, as with all precious things, it is health and medicine. It increases muscular power, it exalts the sex drive, it stimulates the nervous and psychical systems. It renders eloquence easy, it leads to benevolence, to good fellowship, to forgiveness and to heroism.

"Wine exalts the fantasy, makes the memory lucid, increases happiness, alleviates pain, destroys melancholy. It reconciles dreams, comforts old age, aids convalescence and gives that sense of euphoria by which life is made to run smoothly, tranquilly and lightly."

Now, the people of New Orleans have always been fond of their glass. They have less of the puritanical outlook, more of the Latin appreciation of the joys of drinking than other areas of America. Their taverns remain open twenty-four hours a day, seven days a week. Unlike Alabama, where some very peculiar "blue laws" still disgrace the law books, Louisiana has a common-sense attitude toward drinking. (It is against the law to carry your can of beer or cocktail from the bar to a table, or to the juke box in Alabama, and by law, Sunday extends from 2 A.M. to 9 A.M. Monday morning for purposes of drinking!). Perhaps the liberality of New Orleans laws concerning drinking may be traced to a literal following of the Biblical injunction, as expressed in the first epistle of St. Paul to Timothy (5:23): "Drink no longer water, but use a little wine for thy stomach's sake."

The Egyptian *fellahin* — the common folk — are said to spend a third of their lives lifting water. It is doubtful if the people of New Orleans regard their Mississippi water as highly as the Egyptians do the Nile. Captain Philip Pittman, a British engineer of the 48th Infantry Regiment, wrote about the muddy river water in 1770:

"I have filled a half-pint tumbler with it, and have found a sediment of two inches of slime. It is, notwithstanding, extremely wholesome and well tasted, and very cool in the hottest seasons of the year; and the rowers, who are then employed, drink of it when they are in the strongest perspiration, and never receive any bad effects from it. The inhabitants of New Orleans use no other water than that of the river, which, by keeping in a jar, becomes perfectly clear."

Drinking of alcoholic beverages became something of a necessity, then, and the topers of New Orleans gave to the English language the word, "cocktail." The word came into general use about 1808 or 1809. The *Oxford Universal Dictionary* defines cocktail as "a drink made of spirit, bitters, some sugar, etc." Eric Partridge, in his etymological book, *Origins,* adds that a cocktail is "any creature with tail resembling a cock's, hence a lively, cheerful, basically spiritous drink." The Sazerac Company of New Orleans offers us still another variation of the origin of the word, "cocktail." Since New Orleans hosts served their mixed drinks in a double-ended egg cup known as "coquetier," the drink soon took on that label. After the United States bought Louisiana and the American frontiersmen poured into the Crescent City during the early years of the nineteenth century, they had difficulty with French pronunciation, and *coquetier* became "cock-tay" to the newcomers. Time and further alteration reduced the word to its present "cocktail."

In a sense this is a personal book. Recipes for various drinks come from my personal collection and some may not find their favorites included here. On the other hand, I have tried to keep up with the times by adding new recipes and a pot pourri of misceallaneous facts about New Orleans and its libations. I take quite seriously the old Spanish proverb, "Hermano bebe, que la vida es breve:" "Brother, drink up, for life is short."

AN UNIDENTIFIED 19TH CENTURY NEW ORLEANS SALOON
— Courtesy of Leonard V. Huber

7

# Basic Mixologist Tips

The success of your bartending efforts will be commensurate with your use of the best ingredients and exact measurements. Nothing is more ridiculous than the amateur mixologist who boasts of his ability to make the "perfect" drink without regard to these two basic rules. Most drink books have a list of basic measurements commonly used around bars. Here is mine:

| | | |
|---|---|---|
| 1 drop | = | 1 minim |
| 1 dash | = | 10 drops or 1/8 teaspoon |
| 1 teaspoon | = | 6 dashes, 1/8 ounce, or 1 dram |
| 1 tablespoon | = | 3 teaspoons or 1/2 ounce |
| 1 ounce | = | 8 teaspoonfuls |
| 1 pony | = | 1 ounce |
| 1 jigger | = | 1 1/2 ounces |
| 1 wine glass | = | 4 ounces |
| 1 cup | = | 8 ounces |
| 1 split | = | 6-8 ounces |
| 1 pint | = | 16 ounces, or 10 jiggers plus |
| 1 fifth | = | 25 3/5 ounces |
| 1 quart | = | 2 pints, or 32 ounces |
| 1 liter | = | 1.057 quarts, 33 ounces plus |
| 1 Imperial quart | = | 40 ounces |
| 1 Magnum | = | 52 ounces |
| 1 half-gallon | = | 2 quarts, or 64 ounces |
| 1 Jeroboam | = | 104 ounces |
| 1 Rehoboam | = | 160 ounces |
| 1 Methuselah | = | 208 ounces |
| 1 Salmanazar | = | 312 ounces |
| 1 Balthazar | = | 416 ounces |
| 1 Nebuchadnezzar | = | 520 ounces |
| 1 Demijohn | = | varies: 1-10 gallons |

## RANDOM HINTS

As a general rule, do not shake such drinks as are made with clear liquors, such as martinis and manhattans. For those drinks which do require shaking, do the job vigorously with a good shaker and cracked ice sounding the jazz-beat accompaniment to the fruit juice ingredients and the liquor. Shake for at least 15 seconds. Pour quickly to avoid diluting the drink with the ice. In the event you wish a frothy drink, add a tablespoon of egg white to the mixture before shaking.

Which comes first, the chicken or the egg? We may side step an answer on that point, but the following order should be followed when mixing: add the sugar and such ingredients as fruit juice first. Then follow with liquor. When adding soda beverages, such as colas, ginger ale or lemon-lime, add these last.

Certain drinks just taste better when they are served in a properly prechilled glass. The method is simple: fill a glass with cracked ice until it is chilled and then remove the ice. Add the drink and serve immediately. If you want frosted drinks, fill the glasses with water, empty, and place in the freezer.

For Margaritas, which have a "salt frost", dip the prechilled glass in salt and brush off the excess, making sure not to allow the salt to get on the *inside* of the glass. For "sugar frost" dampen the rim of a prechilled glass with a slice of lemon and dip in sugar. Brush off the excess.

The base or fundamental ingredient of a cocktail should generally comprise between half and three-quarters of the volume, including vinous liquors or such aromatic wines as vermouth.

The modifying agent is what the base needs to convert it into a cocktail. Bitters, discussed below, is one type. Fruit juices, cream, eggs and sugar are other modifying agents. Do not let them dominate the drink. They are for accent; not to replace the liquor!

To estimate how much booze to provide for your home entertainment, consider the average person for lunch is going to consume two cocktails, while your cocktail party guests will down on an average of two drinks an hour. Buffet guests enjoy between three and four cocktails, while an evening bash ought to provide four drinks per person.

Among my set of friends, there are two generally-accepted practices: B.Y.O.B. (Bring Your Own Bottle) and the open bar. In the latter case, guests mix their own from half-gallon bottles placed in a convenient location, in proximity to ice, water and mixers. If, on the other hand, you want to play host and mix the drinks for your guests (as well you should!), you can use a convenient scale if you are making standard cocktails which require a jigger per drink (one and one-half ounces). You should be able to get almost seventy cocktails for four fifths, or 85 cocktails for four quarts. Simple arithmetic should give you the *average* amount to have on hand for the expected number of guests, but the wise host always maintains a case or two in reserve against an emergency.

As for the number and variety of glasses you should have for any home bar, there are a number of good books which give you the basics, in particular those by David Embury and Thomas Mario (see appendix: More Reading About Booze).

# Some Historical Highlights on New Orleans Booze

Jenny Lind, the "Swedish Nightingale," once remarked about New Orleans: "In New Orleans, indeed, drinking seems to hold its chief abiding place in the New World, and I suppose that more spurious liquor and more genuine brandy is sold and consumed in this city than in any other part of the Union." If New Orleans has always been known for its drinking habits, the city comes by the reputation honestly, for an examination of the history of colonial New Orleans shows some of the early problems regarding taverns.

Even before the French moved their capital of Louisiana from Mobile to New Orleans in 1718, the French settlers had their taverns. Indeed, Jean Baptiste LeMoyne, Sieur de Bienville, one of the key leaders of French Louisiana, operated a tavern at Mobile between 1706 and 1712. He commanded a relatively high price for his wine of $200 a cask, but Antoine Crozat's agents of the colonizing company forced the price down to $64.00.

At New Orleans in 1746, the thirsty gathered to hear a proclamation signed by Governor Pierre Rigaut, Marquis of Vaudreuil. The number of taverns in New Orleans was fixed at six, in addition to the two canteens established for the French and Swiss soldiers. Licenses to operate taverns were to be sold at public auction to the highest bidder, and the proceeds were to go into a fund for the expenses of the charity hospital. Tavern-keepers were warned not to sell or give liquor to the Indians or to Negro slaves. Monsieur Dusigne bid some 775 *livres* (about $155) for the first license sold, and the total amount for all six taverns was a whopping $921.

Wine-drinking habits of the French colonists may have been one of the chief causes for a political revolt. When the first Spanish governor of Louisiana, Antonio de Ulloa, arrived in 1766 to raise the Spanish colors over New Orleans, he tried to favor the Spanish wine producers who made a red wine similar to the French clarets. In a short time ships arrived with *rioja* wine from Spain, but unfortunately for the industry, *rioja* does not travel well, and the early barrels were a big disappointment to the people. Although other factors contributed to Ulloa's unpopularity and the resulting "Revolution of 1768," when he was forced to board his ship and leave New Orleans, I like to think that the New Orleans preference for the Bordeaux, Burgundy and red clarets of France played an important part.

Alexander O'Reilly re-established Spanish rule in 1769, but the populace grumbled for several years. In 1777, the San Sebastian firm of Larralde sent a ship to New Orleans, where it unloaded 98 casks of Spanish *Rioja*. The wine met with a rude reception. One official wrote, "When the colonists tasted it, they manifested as much repugnance for it as if they had taken an emetic." Boston had its Tea Party, but the people of New Orleans may just as well have had their Wine Party.

As with all mercantilistic nations in the colonial era, Spain sought to drive out foreign competition, and a 1768 royal decree forbade the importation of non-Spanish wines. So intense was the New Orleaneans' love for French wines, however, that in 1782 another edict was passed which permitted French wines to enter New Orleans duty-free. Demand continued, and even during the undeclared naval war between the United States and France in 1798, Bordeaux wine came into New Orleans, but the cost soared from $40 to $100 a cask.

During the Spanish domination of New Orleans (1769-1803) wines were subject to sale at public auction whenever a ship unloaded the barrels near the wharf. Wholesalers and tavern-keepers generally had an edge over the individual buyers because they had the necessary cash to purchase the wines. Moreover, they usually met before the sale and agreed on a fixed price to be paid.

When C. C. Robin visited New Orleans toward the end of the Spanish era, he wrote about the relative popularity of the wines: "The English drink the Madeira and the Spaniards the Málaga, but the French, being the most numerous, insure that the greatest consumption is of French wines. Besides, the Spaniards have adopted our ways and also taken up drinking them and their greater abundance is more conducive to habitual use . . . the consumption of French wines is so great that their abundance never lowers the price for long. One can always make a reasonable profit out of wine," he concluded.

Considering these facts, it is difficult to understand the statement of Robert R. Livingston, the diplomat who helped arrange the sale of Louisiana from France to the United States. He claimed that French wines would not be pleasant to the palates and purses of the Louisiana people!

The people not only loved their wine, but also enjoyed their brandy, despite the high import tariff. Robin wrote that if the price of brandy were lowered, the people would enjoy it more and become accustomed to it. As it was, a locally-distilled fiery, "rot-gut" rum known as tafia was a popular hard liquor. It sold for only a fraction of the cost of imported French brandy, which steadily increased in price from the $4.00 charged for a cask in 1777.

Whiskey was known in New Orleans primarily because of its

export from the western settlements of the United States, particularly Kentucky and Tennessee. "Monongahelie", as it was sometimes known, came from as far away as western Pennsylvania and gets its name from the Monongahela River which, flowing with the Alleghany to form the Ohio, meets at Pittsburgh. Down this river the American frontiersmen poled their flatboats laden with "Bald Face," "Bust-Head," or "The Stranger" — all terms for the strong American whiskey — to the landing at New Orleans. In pretaxation days the whiskey had sold for as little as 50 cents a gallon, but Alexander Hamilton's excise tax and the shortage of whiskey during General "Mad" Anthony Wayne's campaign against the northwestern Indians in 1794, drove the price up to $8.00 a gallon. The New Orleans tariff on whiskey in 1796 was 31 cents a gallon. The repeal of the whiskey excise tax in the United States in 1797 stimulated trade between Kentucky and New Orleans.

Gin was not a very popular libation in colonial New Orleans, but it was possible to buy both Holland and Island gins at 20 and 30 cents a bottle respectively at first. By the end of the Spanish régime, however, gin lovers had to pay a dollar a bottle.

New Orleans' favorite liqueur, absinthe, was available, and thirty bottles sold for $17 in 1777. Cherry liqueur, anisette and hard cider are also mentioned in the ancient documents.

Beer, too, was an important beverage in colonial New Orleans. In 1771 Lieutenant-governor Athanase de Mézières urged the government to subsidize breweries and the manufacture of malt liquors and vinegars. Using the mercantilistic argument, he argued that valuable foreign exchange might be saved if Louisiana produced its own malt products. Marcos Olivares of New Orleans undoubtedly agreed, for he purchased 31 barrels of beer at New Orleans in 1782 for the price of $530. The English traveler, Francis Baily, enjoyed his porter at one inn during 1797, and at a 1799 auction sale, 55 bottles of beer sold for $20.56.

Spaniards have always enjoyed a wine punch, made with a base of *rioja* or *valdapeñas* red wines. This *Sangria,* as it was called, was popular in New Orleans, but apparently some unscrupulous tavern-keepers were too light on the wine and too heavy on the Mississippi water, for a 1775 regulation of the *Cabildo* (city council) forbade the sale of such "punch." Still, by 1797 the law was ignored, and Francis Baily wrote that the people loved to mix their claret and water for a weak punch.

During the early years of New Orleans, two Spanish settlers named Antonio Méndez and Joseph Solis succeeded in crystallizing Louisiana sugar, but it was not until 1794 that Etienne de Boré made a commercial venture out of the sugar. Thereafter, Louisiana

12

was considered one of the most important sugar producers on the mainland of North America. One of the by-products of the sugar industry was the raw *aquardiente de caña* or tafia, a rum-like liquor similar to the head-pounding *trago* of Guatemala. Despite laws against supplying the Indians with tafia, even the government provided the Choctaws, Chickasaws, Cherokees and Creeks with annual subsidies, including generous amounts of tafia.

Mr. Delongua, who distilled tafia near New Orleans in 1799, ordered a 1,500-gallon still, which was carried down the Mississippi on a flat boat. Toward the end of the colonial era, twelve distilleries operated near the city. Observers predicted that one Parisian arpent of land, measuring 185 feet square, would produce an average of 1,200 pounds of sugar and fifty gallons of tafia. Americans looked forward to Louisiana's production of 25,000 hogsheads of sugar and 12,000 puncheons (a large cask containing about 70 gallons each) of tafia.

The French and Spanish masters of Louisiana sought to regulate taverns from the beginning. When Alexander O'Reilly brought Spanish power and laws to New Orleans in 1769, one of his first regulations concerned "Instructions to the Innkeepers, Tavern-keepers, Billiard Parlor-keepers, and the Master Lemonade Seller." Here are a few of the provisions:

"There shall be no more than six innkeepers in this City, in conformity with our aforesaid Ordinance, for the comfort of foreigners and travelers. The innkeepers will give persons who lodge with them wholesome food and drink, and they shall lodge them comfortably, treating them with the attention they are due.

"Likewise, innkeepers shall serve the inhabitants of the city both drink and food when they desire to dine in the establishment, or when they order food or drink brought to their own homes, under fair conditions, in order to prevent any argument over the price.

"Consequently we prohibit all townspeople from being served food and beverage as boarders, unless they reside in that house, under penalty of one hundred *livres* ($20) fine.

"The said innkeepers shall be required to have measures for supplying their beverages, in conformity with the customary measures of the city. They shall not adulterate the liquor they sell, nor serve sour wine to their boarders, nor to the inhabitants who wish to take it home. It is permissible to deliver wine only in bottles, under penalty for violations of one hundred *livres* fine and the loss of said liquor which shall be thrown into the street.

"They are forbidden to give any townsman a drink unless it

13

is during meals; they are, however, authorized to sell to them all kinds of wine in bottles, liquors and brandy, provided that these beverages are consumed outside, under penalty of arbitrary fine."

This regulation of 1769 also established an annual license fee for innkeepers at twenty dollars, payable in four quarterly installments.

The regulations governing tavern-keepers are even stranger by comparison with New Orleans laws of the 70's. Although O'Reilly fixed the total number of taverns for the city in 1769 at twelve, just twenty years later a total of 94 individuals paid a total of more than $2,000 for the privilege of selling liquor. Here are O'Reilly's rules for the taverns:

"No one shall keep any tavern unless they first obtain the government's written permission, under penalty of banishment from this city.

"The tavern-keepers thus provided for shall not lodge people on their premises as boarders. Nor shall they serve persons with table cloths or napkins. They shall restrict their service solely to the sale of liquor, either for consumption on the premises or for being carried out. Exceptions will be made for bread, butter, cheese, oysters, salad, sausages, and radishes, and these may be served to those customers. For other foods served, there will be a fine of fifty *livres*.

"Tavern-keepers shall see to it that they serve drinks in moderation only to those requesting them. They shall not sell liquor on Sundays or Feast Days during High Mass, nor during Vespers, or while the Benediction of the Holy Sacrament is taking place. They shall exclude customers from their taverns during such times under penalty of prison and fifty *livres* fine.

"The tavern-keepers are also ordered to have their doors and windows closed every day at 8 P.M. It is expressly forbidden for them to permit any person to drink there after the time fixed in this article, subject to a fine and imprisonment.

"All persons selling liquor are especially forbidden to sell or give same to Indians, Squaws, Mulattoes, Mulattresses, Negroes or Negresses, who do not have written permission from their masters. As for free savages, it is totally against the law to sell liquor or give it to them under any pretext whatsoever, under penalty of one hundred *livres* fine and eight days in jail. Second offenders will suffer even stiffer punishment.

"Tavern-keepers are warned not to adulterate their liquor nor to sell or deliver sour or stale beverages under any pretext, due to the harmful results of such practices. They shall use honest measures conforming to the city standard weights and measures when measuring out their liquor. They are forbidden from selling unmeasured liquor in bottles under penalty of fifty *livres* fine for first offenders, in addition to the loss of the adulterated liquor, which shall be thrown into the street. Second offenders will be subject to the full prosecution of the law, which declares that the use of false weights and measures is equal to theft.

"Tavern-keepers may sell such beverages as wines of all kinds, brandy, and tafias. They may not sell any fine bottled liqueurs, syrup, cider or beer because these beverages are reserved to the managers of billiard parlors.

"The tavern-keepers and innkeepers granted our permission shall have a sign on their doors bearing their names and showing their licenses. Violators will be dismissed from their professions.

"Tavern-keepers shall pay the sum of 200 *livres* per tavern for their annual licenses, payable in advance at the beginning of each quarter.

"Said tavern-keepers shall report any trouble or fights which occur in their taverns immediately to the police officer. In order to halt such disorders at the beginning, tavern-keepers shall request aid from the nearest guards who are hereby authorized to arrest the guilty parties. Vagabonds, notorious men and women of ill repute are expressly forbidden to enter taverns. There shall be no swearing or blasphemy. Violators of these rules shall be arrested and confined to prison."

In his regulation for billiard parlors, O'Reilly allowed them to sell such bottled liquors as syrup, lemonade, beer and cider, but they were forbidden to sell wine in casks, brandy or tafia. The penalty for violations was the confiscation of the liquor.

A Master Lemonadier was also licensed to operate a cafe in New Orleans where he dispensed "all kinds of lemonade, liquors, fruit brandies, orgeats, syrups, liqueurs, sugared almonds, coffee beans, powder, and brewed coffee, and prepared chocolate." There was a curfew set at 10 P.M., and like the taverns and billiard parlors, they were required to close during church services.

At first the tavern-keepers bought their licenses directly from the government, but by 1775 the business had a middleman. Pedro Moris agreed to become the lessee for tavern licenses by posting a bond of $6,600 and paying an annual fee of $840 to the city. He also donated $100 annually to the charity hospital. Moris drew up a list of New Orleans taverns for a distance of three-quarters of a league from town and was careful to report the existence of any unlicensed taverns in the vicinity to the government.

Tavern licenses increased from an average of $23 per year in 1771 to $40 in 1794. By way of comparison, the United States in 1816 charged an annual fee of $60 plus a $2.50 issuing fee. The money from tavern licenses went to a good cause. Generally it helped orphans and hospitals. Governor Esteban Miró in 1786 decreed that the money collected in fines on tavern-keepers would go to a fund for chamber and justice expenses. At times the money was used to increase the size of the New Orleans Police Department. The Cabildo (city council) in 1797 ordered tavern license fees set aside for the support of the St. Charles Charity Hospital, and one council member urged the creation of six additional taverns and to use the money collected from license fees for hiring two or three more constables.

The large variety of liquors available in Spanish New Orleans may be discovered by checking the 1796 tariff which was established by the Intendent of Louisiana, Juan Buenaventura Morales. The original of this document is located in the Archivo General de Indias at Sevilla, Spain.

## TARIFF ON LIQUOR IMPORTS FOR LOUISIANA
### AUGUST 24, 1796

Note: the *real* was equal to 12½ cents.

| Type of Liquor | Container & Size | Duty in Reales |
|---|---|---|
| Brandy | Dozen bottles | 16 |
| Bordeaux Brandy | Small barrels (*barrilitos*) | 18 |
| Provençal Brandy | Small barrels | 12 |
| Bordeaux Brandy | *Barricas, la velte* or 2 gallons | 8 |
| Provençal Brandy | Same | 5 |
| Rum (*aquardiente de caña*) | Barricas | 80 |
| Whiskey | Gallon | 3 |
| Cherry Brandy | Dozen bottles | 16 |
| Anís | Quintal | 40 |
| Anisette (fine) | Basket of two flasks | 12 |
| Anisette (ordinary) | Basket of two flasks | 8 |
| Kirsch | Dozen bottles | 32 |
| Liqueurs | Bottle | 4 |
| Liqueurs of Provençal and like quality | Dozen flasks | 5 |
| Red Burgundy wine | Barrica | 400 |
| White Burgundy | Same | 180 |
| Red Burgundy | Dozen bottles | 48 |
| White Burgundy | Dozen bottles | 18 |
| Champagne | Dozen bottles | 60 |

| Type of Liquor | Container & Size | Duty in Reales |
|---|---|---|
| Chipre wine | Dozen bottles | 32 |
| Condui wine | Dozen bottles | 24 |
| Madeira wine | *Pipe* of 108 gallons | 880 |
| White or red wine from Cataluña, Valencia & Aragón | *Arroba* | 4 |
| White or red wine from Málaga, Xerez, & rest of Andalucía | *Arroba* | 10 |
| White or red wine from Andalucía | Dozen bottles | 16 |
| Wine from Malvasia | Dozen bottles | 24 |
| Wine from Frontignan | Dozen bottles | 20 |
| Muscatel wine | Dozen small flasks (*frasquitos*) | 8 |
| New red wine from Bordeaux & Cahors | *Barrica* | 112 |
| Old red wine from the same | *Barrica* | 200 |
| Old red wine from the same | Dozen bottles | 20 |
| White Bordeaux wine | *Barrica* | 80 |
| White Bordeaux wine | Dozen bottles | 12 |
| Provençal wine, usually called Costal, Languedoc and Rochelle | *Barrica* | 64 |
| The same | Dozen bottles | 12 |
| Red wine from the Cape of Good Hope | Dozen bottles | 60 |
| White wine from the Cape of Good Hope | Dozen bottles | 40 |
| Moselle & Ringau wines | Dozen bottles | 12 |
| Naples & Portuguese wines | *Pipa* | 200 |
| Corcega wines | *Pipa* | 150 |
| Canary Island wines, called *vidueño* | *Pipa* of 120 gallons | 720 |
| Dry wine from Canary Islands | *Pipa* of 120 gallons | 320 |

Note: To determine net weight from gross weight, deduct 70 pounds for the *Barrica* and 25 pounds for the *Barril*.

[1]Juan Buenaventura Morales, "Tariff," New Orleans, August 24, 1796, AGI, PC, leg. 184-A.

# Eye-openers and Morning-after Remedies

Alcohol is a poison, and if you drink too much the body will react in a variety of unpleasant ways. Your tongue feels as if it has had a furrier install thick rugs over it. Alcohol has the effect of irritating the mucuous membranes of the intestinal tract, which produces catarrh, hyperacidity and fatigue. Upon entering the bloodstream, alcohol proceeds to devour the vitamin $B_1$. Your head throbs. Your stomach is queasy. You are afraid you are dying, and you are afraid you won't die.

The proper method of avoiding the common hangover if you should over-indulge is to take precautions the night before. Alcohol can be eliminated from the system by clearing out the stomach. Drink huge quantities of hot water and induce regurgitation with your finger tip if necessary. Repeat. Finally, drink two glasses of warm water with a bit of aromatic spirits of ammonia or sodium bicarbonate. Take a long walk and help the lungs expel the alcohol. Take a hot shower and perspire some of the alcohol out of your pores.

Despite evidence to the contrary, millions of topers claim that the morning-after eye-opener does work for them! Whether this is purely psychological or not, it gives you the feeling that you are doing something about your condition. Basically, there are two types of eye-openers: non-alcoholic ones and the "hair of the dog" type. First, since alcohol started your trouble in the first place, try these old standbys: milk, tomato juice, clam juice.

If what you want is a bit of the hair, try Ted Shane's 'Hangover Breakfast."

A jigger of the liquor that started you on the road to perdition
One pint of milk
One half-pint of tomato or clam juice
One cup black coffee to which is added a teaspoonful of aromatic spirits of ammonia
Return to bed. Rest, rest, rest.

Another favorite hangover chaser is the *Prairie Oyster,* not to be confused with a cattle delicacy!

1 ounce cognac
1 tablespoonful of vinegar
1 tablespoonful Worcestershire sauce
1 teaspoonful catsup
1 teaspoon angostura bitters

Mix in an old-fashioned glass over a cube of ice. Drop the yolk of an egg into the mixture and a dash of cayenne pepper. Swallow without breaking the egg.

18

A similar remedy is *Old Pepper.*

1 jigger whiskey
½ lemon squeezed
3 dashes angostura bitters
1 teaspoon of either chili sauce or tomato juice
1 teaspoon of Worcestershire sauce
1 dash of Tabasco sauce

Mix thoroughly and serve in a whiskey sour glass. If this doesn't cure your headache, it may succeed in burning out the pain!

Absinthe, Pernod, Herbsaint and similar liquors form the ingredients of many eye-openers. A classic favorite is the *Morning Glory:*

1 jigger Scotch
½ teaspoon sugar
3 dashes lemon juice
3 dashes lime juice
3 dashes Pernod, Herbsaint or similar absinthe type
3 dashes Angostura bitters
1 white of an egg, well beaten

Mix ingredients over two ice cubes in a tall 16-ounce highball glass. Fill with siphon of seltzer or club soda well stirred until drink is frosty. Drink rapidly.

Brennan's Restaurant in New Orleans offers a variety of eye-openers, including the famous Bloody Mary (see vodka section), the Sazerac (see Sazerac section), fizzes (see that section), and various absinthe-type drinks (see absinthe section). A special favorite is the Ojen cocktail. Ojen is a Spanish liquor (pronounced "Oh-*Hane*") which has a distinctive Pernod-like taste. The Ojen cocktail is easy to mix. Simply add 3 dashes of bitters to a jigger of Ojen in a prechilled Old-Fashioned glass. Add ice cubes and sit back.

For a change of pace in your eye-openers, try this one:

## POLYNESIAN PICK-ME-UP

2 jiggers vodka
1 cup chilled pineapple juice
2 tablespoons heavy cream
1 teaspoon curry powder
1 teaspoon freshly-squeezed lemon juice
4 dashes Tabasco sauce

Place ingredients in a blender with cracked ice and blend for 10 seconds at high speed. Pour into prechilled Old-Fashioned glass and dust lightly with cayenne pepper, which adds color and piquancy.

For a Lucullan, Diamond Jim Brady morning-after, if you have the money and time, go to Brennan's for their "traditional breakfast." Have an absinthe suisesse, followed by a fresh Creole cream cheese. Follow with Eggs Benedict and a sirloin steak smothered with fresh mushrooms. Enjoy hot, freshly-baked French bread and marmalëde made with the bitter Sevilla oranges. Savor some crêpes Suzette and some fine, dark roast New Orleans coffee served with hot milk (café-au-lait). Lean back and enjoy a snifter of fine cognac. Ah! Well, nutrition experts do agree that a solid breakfast is the best way to begin your day . . .

Photo from Mrs. Charles L. Coe

AN OLD NEW ORLEANS TAVERN
— Courtesy of Leonard V. Huber

# Absinthe Makes the Heart Grow Fonder?

It's a darned shame that the true absinthe has been outlawed! Throughout the world millions of early risers from France to Mexico and back to Spain used to enjoy their morning nip of absinthe — purely for medicinal purposes, of course. Nothing clears the head, spreads that warm feeling in one's tummy, dissolves the tongue fuzz, and gives you the right start to a day's problems like absinthe. Too bad Jean Lanfray blew it all in 1905!

After his eye-opener of 1 part absinthe to 3 parts water, the 31-year-old Lanfray went on to down crème de menthe, cognac, homemade wine, coffee, and brandy. By the end of the working day, the remarkable Lanfray had tippled almost two gallons of intoxicants. Besides, when he came home, he discovered his wife had not shined his boots. Naturally, he took his rifle and shot her dead! Next he polished off a couple of his daughters and goofed a suicide try. The end result was to blame absinthe for the whole mess. Medical men jumped on the bandwagon and claimed absinthe caused insanity, palsy, baldness, and convulsions. The end result was the death knell of a $100,000,000 absinthe industry.

Absinthe derives its name from the Latin word for one of the numerous herbs which are steeped in neutral grape spirits for eight days before distilling: *Artemisia absinthium*. Even the legal vermouth is said to contain a few drops of absinthol. Known to the ancients for its medicinal qualities — "absinthe is the remedy for all diseases," wrote the Marquise de Sévigné — Switzerland exported some three million gallons of absinthe a year before it was banned.

It is said that the door of opportunity is never closed but that another opens, and Dr. Pierre Ordinaire, was no ordinary man. He concocted an absinthe tonic which combined some fifteen plants, including camomile, persil, spinach, various anise varieties, coriander, melissa herb, hysop and Veronica. He combined these with an infusion of dried absinthium and distilled 136-proof alcohol. When absinthe was banned, his successors in the absinthe business developed the Pernod formula which is imported into the United States *sans* wormwood and at only 90°. Pernod drinks are also made up in France and Spain on the exclusive formula. New Orleaneans buy their Pernod, which is imported from French distilleries of Lyon, Montreuil, Paris, Bordeaux and Marseille.

Pernod may be the most familiar, but there are two varieties also very popular in New Orleans. Jacquin's Liqueur d'Anis is a French product, but is also produced in the United States from the patent by Charles Jacquin of Philadelphia. This 1884 distillery turns out a potent 136-proof liquor, which is very much like the original absinthe. Another liqueur with an anisette base is "La Drink Extraordinaire de Nouvelle Orlfians" — Herbsaint, produced by the Legendre Company of New Orleans.

Devotees of the absinthe-like drink swear by its medicinal uses, particularly for sensitive stomachs. For this reason, it is the component ingredient in many eye-openers. Old New Orleans absinthe drip fans smile indulgently when the uninitiated complains that the drink tastes like paregoric! The following are a few of the most popular drinks, all of which use Pernod, Herbsaint or Anis liqueur.

## NEW ORLEANS LOTUS CLUB

Dissolve a lump of bar sugar with a few dashes of bitters. Muddle in a bar glass. Add a dash of Pernod *(et al.)*. Add a jigger of bourbon or rye. Stir and serve in a prechilled Old-Fashioned glass with a twist of lemon to give it that pungent lemon oil touch.

## ABSINTHE SUISESSE

Brennan's does a good job with this, but so does the Court of Two Sisters.

1 jigger Pernod, etc.
2 dashes anisette (white)
1 pony of water
½ teaspoon bar sugar
the white of one egg

Shake with cracked ice or, better still, put ingredients in a blender and bring to a frothy delight. For a New Orleans morning, follow this with a Creole creamed cheese and some fresh Hammond strawberries.

## ABSINTHE FRAPPE

Similar to the Suisesse above, except that it lacks the egg white and sugar. Use a proportion of 2 parts Pernod to 1 part anisette plus 1 pony of water. Shake with ice and serve in a tall glass.

## HERBSAINT NEW ORLEANS

2 ounces Herbsaint
2 ounces sweet Vermouth
1 teaspoon sugar

Place ingredients with cracked ice in a shaker and give it the business. Strain into a prechilled cocktail glass, or Old-Fashioned glass with twist of lemon.

# HERBSAINT FRANCAISE

In days of yore, the New Orleans absinthe lover would go to the marble-base fountain at the Old Absinthe House, there to gaze fondly as the drip, drip, drip of the never-dry absinthe tap spread the nectar of the gods upon an ice-filled glass, as the loving bartender stirred with a delicate flourish of the swizzle stick. (See p. 76).

To bring a bit of authentic New Orleans to your home bar, why not order a pair of "drip glasses" from Herbsaint? (P.S., Legendre Company, P. O. Box 52821, New Orleans, Louisiana) Now you are ready to make the original Absinthe Drip, or Herbsaint Française, just as it might be done at Brennan's or the Old Absinthe House.

Fill your drip glass with cracked ice. Add two ounces of Herbsaint or Pernod and ½ teaspoon of simple syrup or sugar to the upper drip section of the glass. When the liquid has filtered through, remove the top and serve with a cocktail straw.

# TIGER TAIL

1 jigger Absinthe, etc.
2 jiggers orange juice

Mix and pour over ice cubes in Old-Fashioned glass and garnish with a wedge of lime.

# COFFEE LANFRAY

In honor of the poor Swiss peasant whose motto might have been, "The family that slays together, stays together."

Add ⅓ ounce of Pernod or its varieties to your after-dinner coffee. Do not carry firearms when enjoying this combination!

# SAZERAC — the Authentic New Orleans Drink

It has been written, "The Sazerac is to New Orleans and the Bayou Country of Louisiana what the martini is to Madison Avenue" or the margarita is to Mexico. Some writers trace the Sazerac back to 1850 when it was first concocted of Sazerac brandy, which was distilled by the French firm of Sazerac-de-Forges. In 1852 Aaron Bird opened the Sazerac Coffee House at 13 Exchange Place in the French Quarter of New Orleans. By 1872, the Sazerac House was opened on Royal Street around the corner from the original coffee house on Exchange. New Orleans topers could rest their legs along a bar which stretched for 125 feet and was the professional home for no less than eighteen bartenders.

In time the Sazerac brandy gave way to rye whiskey. No one seems to know just when this departure took place, but when the Roosevelt Hotel opened its Sazerac Bar in 1949, rye whiskey had become the acceptable ingredient. Gradually bourbon came to replace rye, and some writers suggest that Owen Brennan, dean of the Old Absinthe House and father of the founder of Brennan's Restaurant, may be responsible. Today most New Orleans bars use bourbon in their Sazerac.

The legends told about the Sazerac are legion. One northerner, who visited New Orleans for the first time and was served a Sazerac, remarked that the drink had integrity. Following a second round, he agreed with F.D.R. that the South was a vastly misunderstood region. Following a third Sazerac, he was heard to proclaim loudly, "Give me my change in Confederate money!"

An essential ingredient of the Sazerac, as for many cocktails, is the addition of a few dashes of bitters. Now is as good a time as any to speak of the "bitters family."

Perhaps the earliest brand was Peychaud's Aromatic Cocktail Bitters. As with other bitters, it is comprised of alcohol, herbs, spices, water, and coloring to make it look appetizing. During the 1793 Negro slave uprisings on the island of Saint Domingue (present-day Haiti), hundreds of French planters fled with what possessions they could salvage. Many came to New Orleans, where they introduced theatrical performances, but Antoine Amedie Peychaud had a different contribution to make.

He was a pharmacist or apothecary, and he brought with him the recipe for compounding a liquid tonic, he called bitters. Since brandy and cognac were among the most popular beverages in New Orleans at that time, he frequently served his visitors glasses of brandy to which he had added a dash or two of bitters. The motto of the Peychaud firm, L. E. Jung and Wolff Co. of New Orleans, is: "L'amer Peychaud ne penêtre sur passé comme aromatique pour faire les cocktails. En usage dans tous les meilleurs cafés." ("Peychaud Bitters have no equal for flavoring cocktails used in every bar of any prominence."). The gold medals won by the firm throughout the world attest to the truth of their motto.

Outside New Orleans, another brand is probably more famous: Angostura Bitters. It was in 1830 that Dr. J. G. B. Siegert began blending water, gentian, flavors of various sorts, coloring and alcohol (45% by volume) to make up his "amargo aromático" or bitters, as the Spaniards call the product. His home was in Angostura, Venezuela, which had recently won its independence from Spanish rule, and as a result, the name was changed from Angostura to the hero of Venezuelan independence: Ciudad Bolívar. Angostura bitters is now produced off the Venezuelan coast, at Puerto de España in Trinidad. Its producers claim — and not without some truth — that the bitters taken with a bit of water prior to dining will stimulate the appetite, while taken with a few drops afterward, it will eliminate flatulence.

Another popular type of bitters, which is indispensable to many New Orleans mixed drinks is orange bitters, a tasty blend of wine, alcohol, sugar, orange and other citrus peels, tincture of cascarilla, gentian and ginger root, spices and the oil of orange, which is prepared in such a way that its aging in wood brings out the aromatic quality.

Although not called "bitters", Falernum is a spicy sweetening agent which is used in cocktails and in cooking. Originally produced on the island of Barbados in 1749, it combines such flavors as almond with spices, sugar and citric acid. It is only 5% alcohol by volume and it is particularly enjoyable when added to fresh fruits such as grapefruit, or when combined in a spicy barbecue sauce or ham glaze.

Now that we know what absinthe is and what bitters may be used, we ought to blend these two basic ingredients to produce a Sazerac.

## SAZERAC

Start your perfect drink with two, heavy-bottomed old-fashioned glasses. In one, place cracked ice and allow to chill. In the other glass crush a lump of sugar with a bit of water. Add a few drops of Peychaud's bitters and a dash of Angostura bitters. Then add a jigger of bourbon or rye whiskey. Place several ice cubes in the glass and stir VERY GENTLY. This is the secret to a good Sazerac: never, never shake it! Return to the prechilled glass, which you empty of the ice and dash in several drops of Herbsaint or Pernod. Twirl the glass until the absinthe-like liqueur coats the inside, and pour the excess out. Now for the marriage! Strain the whiskey mixture from the other glass into this absinthe-coated pre-chilled glass. A twist of lemon, the oil from which has delicately added its nuance of flavor to your drink, is the last touch, but do not add the lemon peel to the drink, and do not use ice cubes in the glass.

As with all fine drinks, there are variations on the theme of the Sazerac. One combines two ounces of bourbon or rye with ¼ teaspoon of Pernod, ¼ teaspoon of Peychaud bitters, ½ teaspoon sugar, and the lemon peel. Unlike the classic Sazerac mentioned above, this variation suggests that the Pernod be used to coat the inside of the glass, but left in afterward! It also calls for the addition to the finished drink of an ice cube and the lemon which you have twisted.

### The Playboy Club of New Orleans has its own variation:

¼ teaspoon Pernod
1 small sugar cube
2 dashes Peychaud's bitters
1 dash Angostura bitters
1 jigger straight rye
  lemon peel

Pour Pernod into prechilled old-fashioned glass and roll glass until inside is entirely coated. Add sugar, both kinds of bitters and enough cold water to barely cover sugar. Muddle until sugar is completely dissolved. Add whiskey and a large ice cube. Stir well. Twist lemon peel above drink and drop into glass.

If you can't decide between these variations and you want to save time, but still want to enjoy a fine Sazerac, the Sazerac Company has come to your aid. Since 1850 they have been bottling a ready-mixed Sazerac cocktail. You stir the contents with some ice, but then remove the ice cubes and pour into a glass. Add a twist of lemon peel. NEVER USE SHAKER — warns the label!

# Henry Ramos and His Famous Fizz

During the 1890's Henry Ramos originated the fizz which bears his name. Since he owned several taverns, he operated a type of "assembly line" procedure: assistant or apprentice bartenders shook the mixture, but it was the "master bartender" who served them. For many years the Roosevelt Hotel has prided itself on serving the best Ramos Fizz in the world, and it is hard to deny that they definitely produce the best in New Orleans.

To make a successful fizz, you need one of the old-fashioned siphons, which formed such a nostalgic part of the old comedies in the movies. You remember (you do?). The comic would turn to a perfectly-dressed gentleman and turn on the siphon, and the audience would rock with laughter as the seltzer sprayed over the poor dude. Alas, the old siphon may have been a victim of our ever-quickening society, but the fizz misses it! Don't try to substitute the bottled club sodas and still expect a perfect fizz. It can't be done. Your best bet is to get one of those clever $CO_2$ cartridge gadgets which converts regular water into *fresh* bubbly. Make your own siphon. It's easy, and it's fun!

## RAMOS GIN FIZZ

1 jigger gin
1 egg white
1 teaspoon powdered sugar
½ lemon, freshly squeezed
½ lime, freshly squeezed
1 ounce cream (or half-and-half)
3 dashes of orange-flower water

Crush the sugar, lime and lemon juice, and egg white together. Add cream, gin and orange-flower water. The secret to this drink is action — shake, shake, shake. Shake again. When you think the drink is frothy enough, shake some more. Pour into a 6-8 ounce glass. Just before serving add the bubbly water from your homemade siphon (if you can't afford the real siphon!).

A variation of this theme is to substitute orgeat for orange-flower water. As I learned in editing a 1769 New Orleans regulation on serving drinks, orgeat is a sweet, non-alcoholic, almond-flavored syrup. In France it is called orgeat; in Italy, orzata. In the United States, Trader Vic's brand of orgeat syrup is usually available.

Another variation is to use a larger glass — something like the Tom Collins glass — tall, and skinny, holding 14 ounces. After you put in 2 ounces of gin, ½ ounce cream, 2 teaspoons sugar, ½ ounce each of lemon and lime juice, 1 egg white, and ½ ounce orgeat, put all ingredients in a blender and run at high speed with crushed ice for five seconds. After you pour into the glass, fill to the top with your bubbly.

Thomas Mario, whose *Playboy's Host and Bar Book* should be considered something of a modern "classic," gives recipes for as many fizzes as there are people who lean to one or another liquor: apricot, aquavit, bayard, blueberry rum, brandied peach, brandy mint, calvados, Danish gin, Dubonnet, Fern Gully, fraise, gin, golden gin, Japanese, morning glory, orange, Ostend, peachblow, royal gin, rum coconut, rum pineapple, Sloe gin, tequila, and whiskey Curaçao. He also gives this potent recipe for the New Orleans Gin Fizz.

## NEW ORLEANS GIN FIZZ

2½ ounces gin
1 ounce lemon juice
½ egg white
1 teaspoon cream
¼ teaspoon orange-flower water
2 teaspoons sugar
1 slice lemon

Shake ingredients together with cracked ice and strain into tall, 14-ounce glass half-filled with ice. Use your siphon or, if you don't have one, try bottled soda. Garnish with the slice of lemon.

## SLOE GIN FIZZ

1 ounce sloe gin (creamy cap)
1 ounce gin
¾ ounce lemon juice

Shake sloe gin, gin and lemon juice well with ice. Fill a 14-ounce glass half full with ice and strain mixture into it. Fill to top with a siphon of fresh soda water. Stir and garnish with slice of lemon.

# SOUTHERN COMFORT —
## Happy Marriage of Bourbon and Peaches

One special kind of liquor, the 100-proof Southern Comfort, started out as bourbon and added some interesting ingredients along the way. "In the days of the Old South," says its distillers, "a discriminating New Orleans gentleman was disturbed by the taste of even the finest whiskeys. So he 'smoothed his spirits' with rare and delicious ingredients, and Southern Comfort was born." The exact blending is a "family secret," but it is obvious that the mixture contains peaches. It is considered a liqueur, rather than a whiskey, but it may be mixed as if it were a peach-flavored bourbon.

Thanks to a high-level advertising program, Southern Comfort devotees are able to pick up free booklets on how to mix a number of fine drinks, some of which are indicated here.

## NEW ORLEANS

4 jiggers Southern Comfort

2 jiggers unsweetened grapefruit juice

Shake over shaved ice. Strain and serve in an old-fashioned glass.

## SCARLETT O'HARA

Antoine's of New Orleans led the nation in introducing this wonderful way to get your Vitamin C.

1 jigger Southern Comfort

1 jigger cranberry juice cocktail

¼ lime, freshly squeezed

Shake (or use blender) with cracked ice and strain into prechilled cocktail glass. (This one is for you, Harris!).

## HONOLULU COOLER

1 jigger Southern Comfort

½ lime, freshly squeezed

Fill tall 14-ounce glass with crushed ice. Add lime juice and Southern Comfort and fill with pineapple juice. Stir. Garnish with slice of pineapple.

# COMFORT SOUR

1 jigger Southern Comfort
½ jigger freshly-squeezed lemon juice
½ teaspoon sugar

Shake in cocktail shaker with cracked ice and strain into **tulip glass.**
Garnish with slice of orange and maraschino cherry.


# COMFORT COLLINS

1 jigger Southern Comfort
½ lime, freshly squeezed

Mix in tall glass and add ice cubes. Fill to top with **lemon-lime soda**
such as 7-Up. Garnish with cherry.


# COMFORT MANHATTAN

1 jigger Southern Comfort
½ ounce dry vermouth
1 dash Angostura bitters

Stir with cracked ice and drain into long-stemmed cocktail glass. **Add**
cherry.

# Fruit Recipes Betty Crocker Doesn't Know

Louisiana is known for at least two important fruit crops — strawberries and wild black cherries. The strawberries grown in and around Hammond in the southeastern part of the state are famous throughout the nation, and the strawberry preserves are delicious on breakfast toast, biscuits or muffins. If you happen to be visiting New Orleans during April, it might be worth the hour drive to Hammond, where they hold the Southeast Louisiana Agri-Dustrial Futurama each year. Strawberry growers from Tangipahoa and Livingston parishes (counties) vie for prizes at the exhibits for various strawberry varieties submitted for judging, as do those who prepare strawberry cake. Strawberry wine is available throughout the area. If you want an elaborate drink concocted in part with Louisiana strawberries, try

## STRAWBERRIES AMARETTINI

1 quart of Hammond's large strawberries

¼ cup sugar

3 ounces crème de fraises or fraisette (strawberry liqueur)

1 ounce kirsch liqueur

1 cup heavy cream

3 tablespoons sugar

1 teaspoon vanilla

1 large can pineapple chunks, drained (13½ ounce can)

3 ounce package of amarettini (Italian macaroons — very small)

Remove the stems from the strawberries and slice in half lengthwise. Mix the strawberries, ¼ cup sugar, and liqueurs together and marinate in refrigerator for about three hours. Whip cream until it is thick, but not stiff, and add 3 tablespoons sugar and vanilla. When three hours is up, combine all ingredients and toss lightly. Serve ice cold — drink and dessert combined!

Another classic New Orleans fruit drink is Cherry Bounce. Here is a recipe which calls for the use of the delicious wild black cherries which ripen in Louisiana's West Florida parishes during April and May. The late Hermann Deutsch, a New Orleans journalist, obtained this recipe from Mrs. Archie R. Smith, Jr. of Covington, Louisiana:

# CHERRY BOUNCE

½ gallon of ripe, wild black cherries
1 fifth of straight bourbon
2 fifths of vodka
2 pounds of fine granulated sugar
2 ounces pure glycerine

Put all ingredients in a gallon jar and cover the mouth with cheese-cloth. Store in a cool, dark place for six months. Strain mixture and cherries through a strainer or colander to remove the pits. Resulting mixture should be bottled in pint flasks. Do not bottle before the six months have elapsed or you will lose a good deal of the special taste of Cherry Bounce.

# STRAWBERRY WHITE PORT

½ ounce crème de fraises (strawberry liqueur)
4 ounces imported white port wine

Fill a tall 14-ounce glass with ice cubes and add port. Fill glass to within ½ inch of rim with tonic water. Float the crème de fraises on top by pouring it over the back of a spoon held against the inside of the glass. Garnish with slice of lemon and top the drink with a large, whole strawberry, preferably with long stem.

# Sweet Cordial Drinks

Ted Shane wrote in 1950, "Thanks for your welcome, which was cordial, and vice verse." Many New Orleans people prefer a sweet cordial after a scrumptuous dinner rather than a heavy dessert. There are a baffling variety of imported and domestic cordials, liqueurs and fruit brandies, which would require an encyclopedia to do them justice.

Among the principal distillers of cordials in this country, we have Arrow Cordials (which produces 21 different varieties); Leroux & Co. of Philadelphia; Domaine Co. of Philadelphia and Auburndale, Florida; Du Bouchett, produced by Many, Blanc & Co. of Lawrenceburg, Indiana and Fresno, California; Bols, the Dutch brand which is made in this country by Erven Lucas Bols Distilling Co. in Louisville, Kentucky; and De Kuyper, made by John de Kuyper & Son at Elmwood Place, Ohio. These are just a few of the numerous companies making cordials with genuine or imitation flavors, dry or sweet.

The list might have been increased by the addition of a number of the firms producing ready-mixed flavors so that all the bartender has to do is to add liquor. Holland House may be the most famous. This subsidiary of National Distillers makes blackberry, apricot and whiskey sour mixes; side car, manhattan, martini, bloody mary, Mai-Tai, piña colada, margarita, daiquiri, banana daiquiri, old fashioned, gimlet, screwdriver, black Russian, Tom collins, and even a dry mix for the Love Bird! It's a lot more fun to make up your own elaborate after-dinner drinks, for cordials are best served at that time. The following are some of the more popular cordials served in New Orleans.

## POUSSE-CAFE

    1 part maraschino liqueur
    1 part curaçao
    1 part chartreuse
    1 part cognac

Pour carefully in the order mentioned so as to keep the colors separate. For a really special treat, set the cognac aflame before serving and dim your house lights!

## UNION JACK

    1 part grenadine
    1 part maraschino liqueur
    1 part green chartreuse

Pour very slowly so as to keep the colors separate.

# RAINBOW

This is a "purty drink" if it is carefully prepared and slowly poured.

1 part parfait d'amour
1 part crème de Cassis
1 part maraschino liquer
1 part green crème de menthe
1 part yellow chartreuse
1 part curaçao
1 part cherry brandy

Three very popular after-dinner concoctions are the following:

## PINK SQUIRREL

1 part crème de noyeaux (almond liqueur)
1 part white crème de cacao
1 part half-and-half

Shake ingredients with cracked ice and strain into cocktail glass.

## GRASSHOPPER

1 part green crème de menthe
1 part white crème de cacao
1 part half-and-half

Shake ingredients with cracked ice and strain into cocktail glass.

## BRANDY ALEXANDER

1 part brown crème de cacao
1 part brandy
1 part cream

Shake ingredients together with cracked ice and strain into cocktail glass. Some like a bit of nutmeg sprinkled on top.

Several after-dinner drinks are popular in New Orleans:

## LADIES' LUCK

1 part anisette (red or white)
1 part triple sec

Shake together with cracked ice and strain into cocktail glass.

## SCORPION

6 ounces of light rum
6 ounces orange juice
4 ounces lemon juice
1 ounce gin
1 ounce brandy
2 ounces orgeat (orange-water syrup with emulsion of almonds)

Mix the ingredients in a blender with about a half-cup of shaved ice. This recipe serves four people. Warning: do not drink the whole thing yourself!

Some cordials have a nut flavor, such as the crème de noyeaux or noya used in the Pink Squirrel, which tastes like almonds. So, too, does crème d'Almond. Cacao mit Nuss, on the other hand, is a crème de cacao with a distinctive flavor similar to filbert nuts.

Mint-flavored drinks can be made with crème de menthe (white or green, they are virtually the same) or peppermint schnapps. The latter is less sweet, more potent. Many enjoy an after-dinner crème de menthe frappé, which is the green variety served over shaved ice, usually with a small straw.

Kümmel is a clear-colored liqueur which has a strong taste of caraway seeds, which reminds you of good sour rye bread. The aristocrat among the variety is the Allasch, originally made in Latvia.

Coffee liqueurs appear in a variety of brands and tastes, ranging from the Mexican Kahlúa, to the Jamaican Tía María. Jean Lafitte reminds New Orleans coffee liqueur *aficionados* of the privateer who helped Andrew Jackson win the Battle of New Orleans in 1815. Crème de Moka is still another variety. Among the most popular Kahlúa drinks is the

## BLACK RUSSIAN

2 jiggers vodka
1 jigger Kahlúa

Stir with ice cubes and serve in prechilled glass with a straw. Almost makes you believe in Leon Trotsky!

The Kahlúa people have an interesting idea which makes for a fine addition in cold drinks. Brew up a percolator of double-strength coffee and add enough Kahlúa to it to suit your taste. Pour mixture into ice trays and freeze. You can also add a sprinkle of nutmeg or a few dashes of vanilla to suit your taste.

Still another way to serve Kahlúa is to make a mild milk-shake type drink by mixing milk and Kahlúa and shaking with cracked ice, or blending in a blender. This is called a Black Cow.

A New Orleans-style after-dinner drink is the following:

## OPAL

1 jigger chartreuse liqueur
6 jiggers Pernod, or other absinthe-like substitute

Shake with crushed ice and serve in prechilled old-fashioned glass.

I have referred above to several drinks calling for Chartreuse. First developed by the Carthusian monks in Europe, this excellent secret cordial is said to be composed of more than 100 different herbs. Produced as early as 1605 in France, Chartreuse comes in two colors and proofs: 86 proof and yellow; 100 proof and green. When the Carthusian order was expelled from France about 1903, they carried their secret with them into Spain, but connoisseurs still prefer the classic, pre-1903 product.

Banana liqueur is imported or produced in the United States. A fine foreign brand is Sicilian Gold, produced in Marsala, Sicily. This is excellent served plain and very cold, as an ingredient in banana daiquiris, or as an ingredient in the following drinks:

## ORACABESSA

1 ounce banana liqueur
½ lemon, freshly squeezed
½ ounce 151-proof rum
1 slice banana
1 slice lemon

To prevent discoloration of the banana, dip it in a bit of lemon or orange juice. Meanwhile, shake other ingredients together with cracked ice and strain over ice cubes into a prechilled old-fashioned glass. Garnish with the banana and lemon slices.

## BANANA RUM FRAPPE

1 part banana liqueur
1 part light rum
1 part orange juice

Mix ingredients and pour over crushed ice in a champagne glass.

## BANANA DAIQUIRI

1 part banana liqueur
2 parts lime juice
8 parts light rum

Shake vigorously with lots of crushed ice and strain into prechilled cocktail glasses.

A delightful libation owes its existence, as do so many of the really fine cordials, to a monastic order, in this case the Benedictine monks. Begun in the Fecamp abbey in France in 1510, the base of this popular cordial is cognac, with the addition of herbs, roots, and sugar. D.O.M. which appears on the label, is an abbreviation of the Latin phrase, "Deo Optimo Maximo," which means "To God, most good, most great." It is sold straight or mixed with brandy as the famous "B. & B." Both are 86 proof, and are sold in quarts or 23/32 quarts (fifths, really). There are many uses of Benedictine.

# BENEDICTINE

1 part Benedictine
2 parts cognac
1 part freshly-squeezed lemon juice

Combine ingredients with cracked ice and shake. Strain and serve in prechilled old-fashioned glass.

# BRAINSTORM

4 parts rye whiskey
1 part French vermouth
3 dashes Benedictine

Stir, but do not shake. Pour into prechilled glass and garnish with a twist of orange peel.

A "demi sec liqueur" from Italy is Tuaca, which is produced in Livorno (Leghorn). You can make Italian coffee by adding a half jigger of Tuaca to hot black coffee. Here are two additional recipes calling for Tuaca:

# IL MAGNIFICO

1 part Tuaca liqueur
1 part curaçao
1 part half-and-half

Combine ingredients with crushed ice in blender at slow speed for 15 seconds. Pour into prechilled champagne glass and serve after dinner.

# HAWAIIAN SNOW JOB

1 jigger Tuaca liqueur
1 heaping teaspoon of Mele-Koi Hawaiian Coconut Snow mix

Place in blender with ½ cup cracked ice and blend at low speed for 15 seconds. Pour into prechilled champagne glass.

Among the cordials preferred by many Spaniards is Cuarenta y Tres (43), which is made in Cartagena from milk, fruits, sugar and flavors. It is golden in color and is vitamin enriched!

One of the most aphrodisiac of the world's cordials is Damiana, a tasty treat distilled from the damiana plant in Baja California, Mexico. This small shrub, *Turnera aphrodisiaca*, produces leaves which give the cordial its resinous, aromatic taste. Known to the Mexicans before the Spanish conquest during the fifteenth century, its medicinal properties include those of a purgative, diuretic tonic. Because the Damiana cordial acts directly on the reproductive system, it should be used with care. CAUTION! Accidents cause people.

The licorice flavor of anís or anisette appeals to many people. Available in American brands in red and clear, anisette is often used as an ingredient in other drinks, but many people enjoy it straight or frappé. The Anís del Mono, produced in Spain, is among the aristocrats of this genre and comes in sweet and dry, as does Anís Chinchón. It is also used in the

# BALTIMORE BRACER

1 part anisette
1 part cognac
1 egg white

Shake with crushed ice and pour into prechilled glass.

Among the most popular cordials in New Orleans, Galliano is surely a leader. When introduced to the American public in 1960 Galliano liqueur was somewhat of a problem for the McKesson Liquor Company. But in the 1970s, the tremendous success of the Harvey Wallbanger has increased demand for the tasty, colorful liqueur to almost 300,000 cases a year. In addition to the numerous recipes found in free booklets provided by the company when you buy your Galliano, here are some recipes which are popular in New Orleans:

# HARVEY WALLBANGER

1 jigger vodka
4 ounces ice cold, freshly-squeezed orange juice
½ jigger Galliano

Place vodka and orange juice in a blender with cracked ice and blend at low speed for 15 seconds. Pour into prechilled tall glass and float the Galliano on top.

# GOLDEN CADILLAC

¾ ounce crème de cacao
¾ ounce Galliano
¾ ounce cream

Combine ingredients with crushed ice in blender at low speed for 15 seconds. Pour into prechilled deep-saucer champagne glass. This is one of the specialties at Broussard's on Conti Street in the French Quarter.

# YELLOW BIRD

1 jigger light rum
⅓ jigger triple sec
⅓ jigger Galliano
1 lime, freshly-squeezed

Combine ingredients with cracked ice and pour unstrained into a stemmed glass. Garnish with slice of lime.

# JUMP UP AND KISS ME

1 ounce Barbados rum
1 ounce Galliano
¼ ounce apricot-flavored brandy
1 ounce pineapple juice
1 egg white
¼ ounce freshly-squeezed lemon juice

Place ingredients in blender or, shaker with cracked ice and mix. Pour unstrained into 10-12 ounce brandy snifter.

# Reverend Craig's Friendly Potable

In 1789 the Reverend Elijah Craig produced a liquid refreshment on his farm in Bourbon County, Kentucky. Soon it was known as "that whisky from Bourbon County." Today it is just plain bourbon. It is 51% at least based on corn (in contrast to corn whiskey which must contain 80%). There are two major types of bourbon: sweet mash and sour mash. The latter is based on some of the "spent" beer from a previous run, and its most famous brands are probably the Tennessee "sipping whiskeys" produced by the Jack Daniel's in Lynchburg, George Dickel of Tullahoma, and Cascade Distillers of Normandy. Sweet mash bourbon, particularly the brands distilled in Kentucky from the limestone spring water, begin with no left-over mash.

The distilling of whiskey is pretty much the same no matter what country producing it or from which grain. The grain is ground into mash and yeast turns it into alcohol. The alcohol is heated and vaporizes. The whiskey thus produced is then stored in wooden casks. After bottling, many distillers place their run in bonded warehouses for at least four years. This carefully-watched bottled-in-bond is 100 proof, and during its "rest" the distillery does not pay taxes on it.

Whiskey may be spelled Whisky (as George Dickel does with his Tennessee Sour Mash Whisky) or Whiskey (as Jack Daniel's does with his Tennessee Sour Mash Whiskey). There is no rule of thumb, but in general the Irish and the Americans spell it with the "e" while the Canadians and the Scots drop the "e."

American bourbons have finally caught on in the rest of the world. Over the last decade German imports of Kentucky bourbon have risen 200%, and even the sophisticated French were replacing traditional liquors with bourbon.

In 1855 Austin Nichols established the brand, Wild Turkey, which is an especially smooth Kentucky straight bourbon. It is available at 101 proof and 86.8 proof. Southern Comfort, as we have seen above, is a bourbon blended with secret ingredients, one of which is peaches.

As for rye whiskey, it is difficult to find a single straight brand (which has been distilled at 160 proof and aged for at least two years). Rather, we have blends of straight whiskey and blended whiskey. The latter contains about 1/5 to 1/3 straight whiskey and it must be 100 proof. The rest of the blend is neutral spirits. Rye whiskey must be made of a grain mixture containing at least 50% rye grains, along with other American grains such as barley or wheat. Blended whiskey is considered more popular with most

Americans particularly in cocktails, but in the South bourbon is still a favorite.

The Canadians produce a very light whisky *(sic!)* which is high on the list of American favorites. Americans import the 6-year-old whisky which is 86 proof (although Canadians drink an 80-proof product).

In Scotland, barley takes over from corn as the leading ingredient in their whisky. There are numerous light and heavy varieties, and the Scotch sent to America may be a blend of two dozen types. The heavy Scotch has a smoky flavor which comes from its being dried over peat smoke.

The Scots waste no time in their drinking, probably because of the peculiar hours for their pubs. They do not use ice, but prefer taking the shot of whisky neat. Many bars have a "bar whisky" inverted with a special pouring device that measures a jigger precisely. The story is told of the topers of the Nine Tumblers Club of St. Andrews, who were each required to finish off nine tumblers of Scotch toddy (Scotch with a squirt of lemon) and then pronounce properly, the phrase "BIBLICAL CRITICISM." You might try this one at your next evening social!

March 17 is St. Patrick's Day, and Irishmen the world over are wont to raise their glasses in memory of the Irish saint who is credited with having started the Irish whiskey industry. Just as brandy is distilled wine, so whiskey is distilled beer, and that was definitely what the fifth-century St. Patrick was about. Since his time, Irish whiskey has been distilled with mash of barley, wheat, rye and oats. Because of similar pub hours for opening and closing, the Irish toper downs his Irish whiskey neat, or as I have seen many an Irishman do, down a double-jigger of whiskey and chase it with a glass of ale. Few people can get as happy in so short a time as the Irish!

Two delicious liqueurs are obtained from Scotch and Irish: Drambuie and Irish Mist, respectively (and respectfully!). Drambuie is intimately associated with Bonnie Prince Charles, who attempted to win the throne of his ancestors in 1745. His personal liqueur was a closely-kept family secret, but he gave Mackinnon of Skye the secret, and the Mackinnon family left to posterity the delicious liqueur, whose name is old Gaelic for "the drink that satisfies."

Irish Mist also has an interesting history. In 1692 the "cream of Irish fighting men" emigrated to Spain, France and Austria after battle losses at Aughrim, Boyne and Limerick during the so-called Williamite Wars. This was "the flight of the wild geese." In Spain and France these Irishmen formed distinctive battalions to fight against the hated English foes, and during the American Revolution they had an opportunity at the battles of Savannah and Pensacola. It was the "geese" who went to Austria, however, who preserved the ancient secret recipe for blending Irish whiskey and heather honey, which was finally returned to the Emerald Isle at Tullach Mhor, the Offaly home of Irish Mist. It is said that there is a spell to the drink, for the essential herbs are gathered at full moon, accompanied by the proper series of spells and incantations.

The following recipes are based on one and another types of whiskey. American blends are most often used in the manhattan and old-fashioned.

## MANHATTAN

2 parts whiskey
1 part sweet vermouth
2 dashes Angostura bitters

Be careful not to shake this drink in mixing! Pour ingredients over ice into mixing glass and stir lightly and gently. Do not bruise the contents! Strain and serve in a prechilled old-fashioned glass. This makes a sweet drink. For a dry manhattan, use French vermouth. For a medium drink, split the vermouth half Italian, half French.

## OLD FASHIONED

If care is used, this cocktail is one of the finest. Actually, this is not a cocktail at all, but a highball. The secret of fine preparation is not to use sugar but sugar syrup. Use a medium-sized old-fashioned glass containing 5-7 ounces. David Embury offers the following excellent method of concocting your own perfect old-fashioned:

Place 1 or 2 teaspoonsful of simple syrup and between 1 and 3 dashes Angostura bitters in your glass. Stir with spoon to blend. Add about a jigger of whiskey and stir again. Add the equivalent of two large ice cubes which are cracked (not crushed). Fill glass within ⅜ inch of top with whiskey and stir again. Add a twist of lemon after you have twisted it over the drink. Garnish with cherry on cocktail spear and serve with short stir rod or old-fashioned spoon. Experimentation will tell you the exact proportions to use to suit your individual taste. Once you are familiar with mixing this drink, you can be a real professional and vary the syrup and bitters to suit your guests' tastes.

Personally, I prefer my bourbon or Tennessee whiskey over ice cubes in a tall highball with water, but many people like to use lemon-lime soda (such as 7-Up), ginger ale, or the cola drinks. Once you have tried, say, Jack Daniel's Black Label in an old-fashioned glass over ice cubes without any mixer, you may be spoiled for other drinks. Its after-taste and aroma are rarely equalled! And I say this as an *aficionado* of the liquor, not just because I am also a Tennessee Squire!

Another favorite is the

## WHISKEY SOUR

2 ounces whiskey
¾ ounce lemon juice
1 teaspoon sugar

Shake ingredients well with cracked ice and strain into prechilled whiskey sour glass. Garnish with slice of lemon and cherry.

Scotch variations are numerous, but the following have found favor among New Orleans tipplers:

## ROB ROY

1 jigger Scotch
½ ounce sweet vermouth
1 dash orange bitters

Stir well with ice and strain into prechilled cocktail glass. For a festive, holiday note, try a twist of lemon and a brandied cherry. Otherwise, hold the cherry.

## RUSTY NAIL

¾ ounce Scotch
¾ ounce Drambuie

Pour over ice cubes into prechilled old-fashioned glass. Stir. My Michigan friends tell me this is known as a Knucklehead in that part of the country.

## SCOTCH SOLACE

2½ ounces Scotch
1 tablespoon honey
½ ounce triple sec
5 ounces milk
1 ounce heavy cream
⅛ teaspoon freshly grated orange rind

Combine whiskey, triple sec and honey in a tall highball glass and stir until well blended. Add milk, cream and orange rind. Fill glass to brim with ice cubes. Stir.

# SCOTCH SLING

1 teaspoon sugar syrup
2 teaspoons, freshly-squeezed lemon juice
3 ounces Scotch

Combine ingredients in a large highball glass and fill with a siphon or bottled soda water.

# PRINCE EDWARD

1 jigger Scotch
½ ounce Lillet (a French Apértif wine with a slightly orange taste)
¼ ounce Drambuie

Shake ingredients with cracked ice and strain over rocks in prechilled old-fashioned glass. Garnish with slice of orange.

The following drinks call for Irish whiskey. Old Bushmill's and John Jameson brands are available in the United States at 86 proof; both are blends.

# KERRY COOLER

2 ounces Irish whiskey
1 jigger dry Madeira (Sercial) or Sherry (Amontillado)
1 ounce orgeat
1 ounce freshly-squeezed lemon juice

Pour ingredients into tall highball glass and add ice cubes. Stir well and fill with club soda. Stir again. Add slice of lemon.

# IRISH ALEXANDER

½ jigger Irish whiskey
½ jigger Kahlúa or other coffee liqueur
½ jigger heavy cream

Shake all ingredients well with cracked ice and pour into prechilled old-fashioned glass. Fill with ice cubes.

# IRISH LUCK

1 jigger Irish whiskey
½ jigger Irish Mist
1 jigger orange juice
½ jigger lemon juice
1 teaspoon bar sugar

Pour ingredients into blender with cracked ice and blend at high speed for 20 seconds. Pour into prechilled old-fashioned glass. Add ice cubes and garnish with a maraschino cherry.

# IRISH ALMENDRA

1 jigger Irish whiskey
½ jigger orange juice
½ jigger lemon juice
2 teaspoons orgeat

Shake all ingredients in shaker with cracked ice. Strain into prechilled whiskey sour glass and sprinkle a teaspoon of toasted almond slices on top. Something different!

For our many friends from Canada who visit New Orleans annually, I include the

# QUEBEC

1 jigger Canadian whisky
¼ ounce Amer Picon
¼ ounce maraschino liqueur (or grenadine if you don't have it)
½ ounce dry vermouth

Shake well with cracked ice and strain into prechilled, sugar-frosted cocktail glass.

# "The Happy Accident" — Brandy or Cognac?

In April, 1779 Boswell wrote in his *Life of Johnson,* "Claret is the liquor for boys; port for men; but he who aspires to be a hero must drink brandy." The word brandy comes from the Dutch, *brandewijn,* which is literally "burnt wine." And that is exactly how brandy came into being — the happy accident.

About the time the Pilgrims put into Cape Cod because they had run short of beer, the French wine trade with Scandinavia had declined, and this led to the accumulation of a large surplus of wine along the Charente River. One Chevalier de la Croix Marron decided to "burn" some of his surplus wine. That is, he put the thin, acidic wine through a rudimentary pot still and tasted the result — bad! So he did it again, and *voilà,* he had produced one of the earliest brandies in France.

Now, all brandy is not cognac, but all cognac is brandy. What is generally served throughout France as *brandy ordinaire,* is really marc, which is a distillation made from the residue of grapes, stems and skins after the wine has been pressed. The distillation of French cognac is rigidly controlled. It comes from the Charente area on the west coast of France north of Bordeaux. The Saint-Emilion grapes of the area — not to be confused with the Bordeaux grape area of the same name — must be distilled twice in pot stills and aged in oaken casks made laboriously by hand (one per day) from a special type of oak obtained in forests of Limousin oak in Limoges.

Old-fashioned techniques are used because trial-and-error has convinced the cognac distillers that they are best. Thus, copper stills are preferred over modern, steel ones. In the hand-made barrels, each stave is cut by hand and skillfully tapered so that they fit together without the use of nails. They generally hold about seventy-two gallons. Cognac is aged in the casks while it absorbs the tannin flavor and turns from gold to a dark chestnut. Cognac evaporates quickly, as much as 10% during the first year, and it is estimated that some ten million bottles of cognac go for the "angels' share" each year; that is, they evaporate into the surrounding air. Barrels are thus topped every year by adding cognac of the same age and quality and by transferring the cognac into older "red" casks, which have lost much of their tannin flavor.

After five years of aging in the cool darkness, the cognac taster selects various "runs" by odor and taste and makes a blend. Straight cognac is to blended cognac as a single melody is to a full orchestrated symphony. Once the cognac is bottled its aging stops for all practical purposes. Thus, a Napoleon Brandy which was bottled in 1815 would not satisfy the palate when consumed in 1973.

Another popular brandy of France is Armagnac, which is produced in the province of Gascony. It is aged in casks made from local Armagnac oak, and its production is likewise rigorously regulated. The best Armagnac approaches the essence of the best cognacs, but some connoisseurs consider it the "poor man's cognac." As in all things regarding taste, you should make up your own mind.

Among the great French firms exporting cognac are Martell, Hennessy, Courvoisier, Hine, Polignac and Remy Martin. A single-cask cognac available in the United States is bottled by Marcel Ragnaud, but it may not please your palate as much as a blended cognac.

The system for grading cognac employs stars and/or initials. Although they are not consistent, nor do they assure you of any special quality or taste, here are the usual meanings:

One Star: aged three years
Three stars: aged five years
V.O.: Very Old
V.V.S.O.P.: Very, Very Superior Old Pale
X.O.: Extra Old
V.S.E.P.: Very Superior Extra Pale

At the risk of attracting the enmity of francophiles the world over, I think that the Spanish brandies are superior to the French ones. (Remember, there is no sense of arguing about taste!). In Spain the coñac or brandy is produced by the same age-old firms which also have made southern Andalucía — particularly the provinces of Xerez and Cádiz — the center of Spain's sherry industry. (A footnote to linguistics: in the Middle Ages the "x" in Spanish was pronounced rather like the Nahuatl "x" of pre-Columbian Mexico, that is, as "sh". Xerez was thus, "sherr-aith", and in time, the English converted it to its present Sherry).

The Spanish brands have found increasing favor in the United States, and several brands are now found in New Orleans liquor stores. Few connoisseurs would disagree that Lepanto is the *crème de la crème* of Spanish brandies, but I developed a taste for the Pedro Domecq brand which is among the most popular in Spain: Fundador. Other brands which are popular are 103, Soberano, Veterano, Centenario, Príncipe, Carlos I, Carlos III, Insuperable, Byass 96, Carabela Santa María, Magno, Larios 1866, and Terry I.°

Of course, France and Spain are not the only countries which produce fine brandies. The Pisco of Peru is popular, and Mexico produces a head-pounding equivalent. Greece is known for its dark

Metaxa. In recent years the California brandy industry has finally come into its own, and in taste, color and aroma, it compares favorably with those of France and Spain.

An old German proverb says, "Brandy is lead in the morning, silver at noon and gold in the night." After a fine dinner, few pleasures can surpass the leisurely enjoyment of a good cigar and a brandy. If you are one of those *torula compagniacensis* (a living organism which is nourished by the fumes of good brandy; actually, a miscroscopic black fungus which grows on the buildings where cognac is distilled in France) you should learn the proper ritual for enjoying a fine, after-dinner cognac.

First, you need a brandy snifter or inhaler, which is an egg-shaped, stemmed glass with a small opening at the top. Your hand nestles the filled glass (just a jigger in the bottom!) as you hold it to the light and remark on its golden beauty, *"quelle beauté!"* As your hand warms the contents, place the glass near your nose and gently savor the aroma. With your eyes almost closed, declare, *"Quel bouquet, quel arome!"* Warm the brandy with your palm again and sip gently — never gulp — and allow a small amount to explore your mouth, slowly so that by the time you are ready to swallow, the brandy has already evaporated. Smile, and whisper gratefully, *"Quel goût!"* By George, I think you've got it!

There are also a number of excellent true fruit brandies available in the United States, all of which offer a different, but enjoyable, after-dinner drink. They are not as sweet as the cordials, but such fruit brandies as Zwack's blackberry, apricot, raspberry, and pear brandy have a delightful after-taste. Because they are fairly expensive by comparison with cordials, they are often combined with such bases as vodka, rum or gin.

Here are four popular New Orleans drinks which are made with cognac or brandy:

## STINGER

The ingredients are brandy and white crème de menthe. The proportions vary, but most prefer the 50-50 ratio. For a dry drink, increase the brandy up to 4-to-1 compared to the crème de menthe. The stinger should be served in a well-chilled old-fashioned glass, but first you must combine the ingredients with cracked ice and stir until the shaker is icy. Sometimes this drink is served with a glass of water on the side. The name "stinger" is apropos, so use caution in the quantity of stingers you down!

# SIDE CAR

8 parts cognac or fine Spanish brandy
1 part Cointreau or Triple sec
2 parts freshly-squeezed lemon juice

Shake vigorously with lots of cracked ice and strain into prechilled cocktail glasses. Add a twist of lemon.

# ALABAMA

1 jigger brandy
1 teaspoon Curaçao
½ ounce lemon juice
½ teaspoon sugar

Sugar frost a cocktail glass after chilling. Combine ingredients in shaker with cracked ice and shake. Strain into glass. Twist an orange peel and drop into glass.

# CALIFORNIA DRIVER

1 jigger brandy
orange juice

Combine in tall glass over ice cubes. The California brandy industry highly recommends this pleasant variation of the screwdriver.

# BRANDIED PINEAPPLE

This is one of my favorites. The better the ingredients, the better the finished product, which makes delightful gifts for your friends, who like to serve it on ice cream.

Cut a fresh pineapple into thick slices. Peel and remove eyes and core. Cut slices into small chunks or strips. Measure pineapple and place in a crock. Add an equal amount of sugar and two ounces of brandy for each cup of pineapple. Mix well and cover. Stir at least once a day so that the sugar will melt and blend with the fruit and brandy. Keep in the crock a month, stirring each day, and then place in canning jars and fasten the lids. Other fresh fruit, canned fruit, and even dried fruit may be substituted, as may rum, bourbon or other whiskey for the brandy.

## "It's Gin, Gin, Gin That Makes You . . ."

Many of us recall the old fraternity song which made its way into many a lad's and lassie's college background:

"Oh, it's gin, gin, gin

"That makes you want to sin

"In the halls, in the halls . . ."

According to legend, the word gin comes from the French name for the juniper, *genièvre*. Four of the principal varieties of gin are English or London dry gin; Holland gin (Zer oude geneve, Schiedam or Schnapps, for example); Old Tom; and Sloe Gin. Actually, Sloe gin is not a gin at all. It is a liqueur distilled from the sloe plums of the blackthorn plant.

Perhaps the most famous cocktail of all is made with gin. I refer to the Martini. Even the word seems to evoke poetic praise:

"There is something about a Martini,

A tingle remarkably pleasant;

A yellow, a mellow Martini;

I wish that I had one at present.

There is something about a Martini,

'Ere the dining and dancing begin,

And to tell you the truth,

It is not the vermouth —

I think that perhaps it's the gin."

—Ogden Nash

The Pulitzer Prize-winning historian, Bernard De Voto, also appreciated a good martini, as he wrote in 1951, "You can no more keep a martini in the refrigerator than you can keep a kiss there. The proper union of gin and vermouth is a great and sudden glory; it is one of the happiest marriages on earth and one of the shortest-lived."

Since virtually everyone loves a good martini, it stands to reason that the formula for making a perfect concoction is easy, right? WRONG! Two equally distasteful extremes have developed in formulating the martini, each with its own accompaniment of bad jokes. There is the wishy-washy school which blends half gin and half vermouth. On the other extreme is the "rinse method" in which vermouth is used to coat the inside of the glass, after which ice-cold, straight gin is added. What a crime; a plague upon both your houses!

49

Most people prefer a blend of 5-to-1, gin to vermouth, and if you are a real toper, a 7-to-1 ratio is permitted. But the 12-to-1 martini is just too, too much! No wonder martinis got such a bad reputation. Certainly the little town of Martinez, California, where the cocktail is said to originate, would not approve of the latter!

As with all good cocktails, the secret of a good martini is to use good liquor. A good French vermouth such as Noilly Prat is suggested. Gin comes in all varieties, but the more expensive imported varieties are really worth the cost. Tanqueray is considered somewhat "heavy" among the imports, while Beefeater's is a lighter variety. Again, suit your taste by trying various brands.

The vermouth is an essential ingredient in a martini because it conceals the harsh, tinny taste of some gins. To offer your guests an interesting variation, however, try Spanish dry sherry such as Tío Pepe in place of the vermouth, for sherry can mask a bad gin and make a fine marriage with a good gin. Make sure you keep your ingredients well chilled. Ideally, mix the martini and place in refrigerator several hours before serving so that the gin and vermouth can get to know each other. After you open a bottle of vermouth, it is a good idea to keep it in the refrigerator, too, in order to keep the aromatic herbs from going flat.

Besides the Martini, gin lends itself to a variety of different drinks. Among the most popular in New Orleans are the following:

## PINK GIN

2 ounces gin

2 dashes angostura bitters

Blend well and serve up or with ice in prechilled glass.

Sir Francis Chichester nipped on this one on his 'round-the-world sail.

## PINK LADY

1 jigger gin

¼ ounce lime juice

1 teaspoon cream

½ egg white

1 teaspoon grenadine

Shake well with ice and strain into prechilled glass. For the professional touch, frost the glass with grenadine and sugar.

# MORRO

1 ounce gin
½ ounce dark rum
½ ounce lime juice
½ teaspoon sugar

Shake well in shaker with cracked ice. Strain into prechilled, sugar-frosted glass.

# SINGAPORE SLING

1½ jiggers gin
1 pony of Kirsch (cherry pit brandy)
¼ lemon or ½ lime, freshly-squeezed
1 teaspoon simple syrup
  dash angostura bitters
1 pony Benedictine (optional)

Shake with cracked ice and strain into tall highball glass. Add ice cube and fill glass with charged water or ginger ale to taste. Garnish with slice of orange and maraschino cherry.

# FOGGY DAY

1 jigger gin
¼ ounce Pernod
1 slice lemon

Shake gin and Pernod with ice and strain into prechilled old-fashioned glass. Add two ice cubes. Rub outside of rim with slice of lemon peel and drop peel into glass. Garnish with lemon slice.

# RED BARON

1 jigger orange juice
1 jigger gin
½ lime, freshly squeezed
¾ ounce grenadine

Mix with cracked ice and serve in prechilled old-fashioned glass.

# BRONX

1 part French vermouth
1 part Italian vermouth
2 parts dry gin
  juice of ¼ orange

Shake with cracked ice and strain into prechilled cocktail glass. Variations include the Bronx Silver (made with the white of an egg) and the Bronx Golden (made with the yolk of an egg).

# DUBONNET COCKTAIL

Here's a drink my father has come to enjoy. He suggests using a light gin such as Bombay, rather than the heavier Tanqueray.

⅓ gin
⅔ Dubonnet

Mix with lots of ice and pour into prechilled, old-fashioned glass. Add twist of lemon.

# MARTINEZ

This is said to be the original and authentic martini, having originated in Martinez, California. For my good friend, Raymond J. Martinez:

2 ounces gin
½ ounce dry vermouth
½ teaspoon maraschino liqueur
2 dashes orange bitters

Stir well with ice and strain into prechilled cocktail glass.

# GIBSON

This is simply a variation of the garnish. Martinis use the olive; gibsons, a cocktail onion.

# SAN SEBASTIAN

1 ounce gin
¼ ounce rum
½ ounce grapefruit juice
¼ ounce curaçao
½ ounce freshly-squeezed lemon juice

Shake well with ice and strain into prechilled cocktail glass.

# Yo, Ho, Ho, Admiral Vernon

In his 1883 classic, *Treasure Island,* Robert Louis Stevenson penned the following ditty:

"Fifteen men on the Dead Man's Chest —
Yo-ho-ho, and a bottle of rum!
Drink and the devil had done for the rest —
Yo-ho-ho, and a bottle of rum!"

Although most colonial powers — England, France and Spain for example — forbade giving Indians rum, our ancestors generally ignored the restrictions. Indeed, white man's fire water, *aguardiente de caña,* tafia, and the whole gamut of distilled molasses drinks, were formidable factors in our conquest of the frontier from its original denizens. A drinking song, said to have originated at Dartmouth, harkens back to those halcyon days of early New England and the English techniques for educating and evangelizing the red man:

"O, Eleazer Wheelock was a very pious man;
He went into the wilderness to teach the Indian,
With a *Gradus ad Parnassum,* a Bible, and a drum,
And five hundred gallons of New England rum . . .
Eleazar was the faculty, and the whole curriculum
Was five hundred gallons of New England rum."

Rum was an essential commodity aboard naval vessels, and we derive the term "grog" from the practice of Admiral Vernon in 1740 of serving rum diluted with water to his thirsty crew. When people from the North visited New Orleans, they carried with them a thirst for grog, but one writer warned that rum was poison in the warm Louisiana climate. A "groggy" person, who is a bit unsteady, may have got that way from drinking too much grog!

Along the Ohio and Mississippi rivers from early times it was the custom to grant sailors and oarsmen, who maneuvered their craft against the treacherous currents, a rum break. The French gave a name to this practice, *filet,* and it was continued during the Spanish period. One Spanish governor, Manuel Gayoso de Lemos, referred to the practice as *"fumando la pipa"* — smoking the pipe! Ships in the Spanish Squadron of the Mississippi readily supplied their crews with periodic rum breaks or *filets.*

But rum given to the Indians led rapidly to their downfall. The British engineer, Captain Philip Pittman, claimed in 1770 that the Tunicas tribe of Louisiana had all but been exterminated by rum. Another visitor to New Orleans three decades later wrote about a drinking party he witnessed:

> "Outside of the gate we saw a large circular shade for drying and manufacturing bricks, under which were upwards of fifty Indians of both sexes, chiefly intoxicated, singing, drinking, rolling in the dirt, and upon the whole exhibiting a scene very disgustful. We soon came to another company of ten men sitting in the middle of the road, all intoxicated, amongst them was one standing, with a bottle of rum in his hand, whose contents he alternately administered to the rest, first by shaking the bottle and then pouring part of its contents into their mouths."

Indians obtained the rot-gut tafia easily and its cost was low. The government supplied such tribes as the Chickasaws with annual presents in an effort to maintain their friendship and support against emigrating frontiersmen. One annual list shows that 660 *potes* (a pot was roughly two quarts) of tafia, valued at 81 cents a pot, were included in the gifts.

Rum comes in a large variety of colors, aromas and proof. Before Fidel Castro in Cuba, most of the rum consumed in New Orleans was made by the Bacardi enterprises in that country, but Bacardi still distills excellent Puerto Rican rums of various grades. It also has distilleries in other countries such as Mexico and Spain. The Puerto Rican rums because of their light quality, have found increasing acceptance in the American market because they will mix with practically anything. The Puerto Rican rums are aged at least a year. During a recent trip to Schwegmann's, a grocery-variety chain in and around New Orleans, I noticed the following Puerto Rican brands for sale: Ron Carioca, Ron Bardinet, Don Q., Ronrico, Bacardi, and Don Matusalem.

Just east of Puerto Rico are the Virgin Islands, the rum from which adds to the buyer's choices. Virgin Island rum is also light, but with somewhat more of a molasses suggestion than the rums of Puerto Rico.

Puerto Rican and Virgin Island rums which are aged at least three years, and some up to six years, are slightly fuller bodied and darker, with a heavier flavor. These añejo, or aged rums, are equivalent to fine cognac, and many connoisseurs prefer to take them in a brandy snifter.

Jamaica rums are even darker in color and are an essential ingredient for Planter's Punch. One of the most famous brands is Myers, which began on Jamaica at Kingston in 1879, and is still produced by the Myers Rum Co. in the Bahamas.

Demerara rum is a special treat. It tests at 151 proof and like the *añejo* rums, it can be taken neat. It is usually floated on top of drinks and lit, as you would brandy. Many travelers to Mexico bring back the basket-covered gallons of demerara rum.

Not usually encountered in New Orleans liquor stores, Batavian arak is a pungent, dry, aromatic rum distilled on the island of Java. Equally rare are rums produced on Haiti, the Hawaiian Islands, and New England rum. The last-named was partially responsible for the illegal slave trade between New England, Africa and the West Indies during the colonial period. New England distilled rum from imported molasses and shipped it to Africa to pay for slaves, which were then sent to the French and Spanish West Indies. These foreign islands in turn, shipped molasses and specie (gold and silver coins) to New England. From these Spanish pesos, or pieces-of-eight, we developed our coinage system based on 100 centavos to the peso or dollar. We still sing, "Two-bits, four-bits, six bits, a dollar . . ." The bits referred to were called rials after the Spanish *reales,* and each "bit" or "real" was worth 1/8 of a dollar, or 12 1/2 cents.

The following drinks are made with rum:

## ZOMBIE

2 ounces light Puerto Rican rum
1 ounce red Jero Passion Cocktail mix (available in New Orleans)
½ ounce freshly-squeezed lime juice
1 teaspoon brown sugar

Blend in electric blender until well mixed and serve over cracked ice in a 13-ounce chimney glass. Garnish with slice of lime, stick of pineapple, and maraschino cherry. Insert two colored straws.

## PLANTERS' PUNCH

1 teaspoon sugar
½ lime, freshly-squeezed (lemon may be substituted)
2 ounces dark Jamaican rum
  dash bitters
  dash grenadine

Shake with ice and pour into tall glass. Add freshly-siphoned soda water to taste.

# BARBADOS PLANTERS' PUNCH

2½ ounces *añejo* rum
½ ounce dark Jamaican rum
1 ounce freshly-squeezed lime juice
2 teaspoons sugar
3 dashes angostura bitters

Place ingredients in a tall 12-ounce glass and stir until sugar is dissolved. Fill glass with cracked ice and stir again. Sprinkle with nutmeg and garnish with a slice of lime.

# TURTLE

¼ lime
1 jigger rum
¼ jigger apricot brandy
   pineapple juice

Pour ingredients over ice cubes into a chilled glass and fill to top with pineapple juice. Serve with straw.

# RUM PUNCH

1 fifth of light Puerto Rican rum
1 cup cranberry juice
1 cup orange juice
1 cup strong tea
2 ounces sugar
12 whole cloves

Add ice cubes and lemon slices and mix in large punch bowl. Serves 15.

# NAVY GROG COCKTAIL

1 ounce light Puerto Rican rum
1 ounce dark Jamaican rum
1 ounce demerara rum (151 proof)
¾ ounce freshly-squeezed lime juice
¾ ounce grapefruit juice
¾ ounce sugar syrup

Mix ingredients with cracked ice and pour into a 14-ounce grog glass. Add straw and garnish with slice of lime.

# BAROCO

1 jigger unsweetened grapefruit juice
1 jigger cherry-flavored brandy
1 jigger light rum

Shake with cracked ice. Serve in highball glass over ice cubes, garnished with slice of grapefruit and cherry. Back in my university days in Mexico City, my friend John Baroco developed this drink, and since he did not patent it, I include it here with my thanks for all those Baroco-and-spaghetti evenings!

# ¡ VIVA MEXICO! — Tequila, Pulque and Other Cactus Juice

During 1954 I had the wonderful opportunity of studying in Mexico, thanks to a grant-in-aid from the Mexican government. Although my primary interest was in Mexican history and government, I was also introduced to the liquid refreshments which are derived from one or another plants of the *agave* family, especially the *maguey.* Long before the conquest of Mexico by Spain during the sixteenth century, the indigenous peoples fermented the "honey water" taken from the maguey plant to make a type of beer called pulque. Not that the pre-Columbian Mexicans were drunks, for the use of pulque was rigorously regulated. Only the sick, the privileged, and senior citizens (over the age of 52!) were permitted their three cups daily. But exceptions were made at festival time, when everyone was allowed a drink or two. Drunkenness led to the loss of one's hair for the first offense. A second-time offender lost his job and his house. There was only one third-time offense, for "habitual drunks" were sentenced to die as being incorrigible.

Many parties in Mexico today serve pulque instead of punch. It is cured with such fruits as strawberries, pineapples and mamey, which give the milky-white liquid a color as well as a slightly different taste. Indians poling their canoes through the so-called "floating gardens" of Xochimilco and Milpa Alta still carry their jars of pulque with its trenchant aroma, so reminiscent of the stable! Because numerous children carried pulque to school to enjoy with their tortillas and beans, authorities sought to prevent the growth of alcoholism by banning the drink. Almost imme- the children developed malnutrition signs and diseases such as beri-beri and scurvey. Chemists who analyzed pulque realized why: it is a natural vitamin tonic, very rich in vitamins A, B and C. More than thirty different foods and drinks can be made from the *maguey* plant, which, taken together with its other uses as fencing, needles-and-thread, cattle feed, etc., make the *maguey* one of the most useful plants known to man. No wonder the ancient Mexicans had a special goddess of pulque!

In the Mexican state of Jalisco there is a town not too far from Guadalajara which has given its name to a distilled form of pulque famous throughout the world: Tequila. It is not fair to call tequila "cactus juice", and its fiery reputation is undeserved. Like rum, there are good tequilas and bad tequilas. It is distilled at 104 proof, and some distillers age it in wood, in which case it becomes *añejo,* or aged, with a golden color. When shipped to the United States, tequila has been cut to either 80 or 100 proof in the bottles. White tequila is aged just a few months in Mexico, but another 18 months in the United States. Gold tequila is aged much longer in Mexico.

Drinking tequila is a ritual, as basic as the cognac ritual is to connoisseurs of that *eau de vie*. I like the way I was taught in Mexico. In the fleshy part of the left hand between the forefinger and thumb, place some salt. Grasp a wedge of *limón* in the same hand. The *limón* is not a lemon, not really like our Persian limes. It is closest to the Florida Key Lime — small, greenish-yellow, and juicy. In the right hand take a jigger of straight tequila. Lick the salt with your tongue, down the tequila and "chase" it with a squeeze of *limón*. There are, of course, variations to this ritual, some preferring the salt and the lime juice before the tequila.

If you have had several of these tummy-warmers, you know why Mexicans love the story about the rat and the cat. It seems that a cat had been badgering the rat so badly that the rat's nerves were shot. He downed several shots of tequila (á la the style just mentioned), drew himself up to his full, belligerent height, staggered to the hole and shouted, "Bring on the goddam cat!"

Another variety of "cactus juice", preferred by some Mexicans over tequila, is *mezcal*. To make a big hit with your friends (?), next time you visit Mexico, bring back a bottle of "Mezcal Legítimo de Oaxaca." It is not generally sold in the United States, and if you look at one of the bottles you will understand why. Inside the "true" *mezcal* is a pickled, real worm of the type that is found on the *mezcal* cactus. *Mezcal* comes with a little bag containing salt-and-cayenne pepper. Dabbing a bit of this on the tongue and then swallowing a shot of *mezcal* can be a very warm experience! I recall one of my friends telling me about living in Arizona and having unwelcome guests arrive periodically to drink up his small stock of liquor, never bringing any of their own. To even the score, he cleaned out the liquor cabinet, made several trips to Mexico and brought back bottles of *mezcal*, each containing its worm. As the bottles were consumed, the worms were poured into one special bottle, so that in a short time, the bottle was half filled with *mezcal*, half with worms. When the free-loaders came next, they were shown the lone bottle of *mezcal* and asked to "help themselves." The lesson was successful!

While *mezcal* should be drunk straight, tequila has found acceptance in a variety of drinks, many of which are found in New Orleans.

# MARGARITA

1 jigger tequila
⅓ jigger triple sec or curaçao
½ ounce freshly-squeezed lemon or lime juice

Shake well with ice and strain into a salt-frosted, prechilled cocktail glass. Garnish with twist of lime or lemon. To salt-frost your glass, rub outside rim with lemon peel and dip into salt. Shake off excess salt and make sure you don't get any on the inside of the glass.

# FROZEN BLACKBERRY TEQUILA

1 jigger tequila
1 ounce blackberry-flavored brandy
½ ounce lemon juice

Put ingredients in blender and mix at low speed for 15 seconds. Pour into prechilled old-fashioned glass and add ice cubes to fill glass. Garnish with slice of lemon.

# TEQUILA DUBONNET

1 jigger tequila
1 jigger red Dubonnet

Pour into prechilled, old-fashioned glass and add cracked ice to fill. Garnish with lemon slice.

# BUNNY BONANZA

1 jigger tequila
1 ounce apple brandy
½ ounce freshly-squeezed lemon juice
½ teaspoon curaçao
1 teaspoon sugar

Shake tequila and other ingredients with cracked ice and strain into prechilled, old-fashioned glass. Add ice to fill glass and garnish with slice of lemon. First devised by the mixologist at the Playboy Club in Detroit.

# CHAPALA

1 jigger tequila
½ ounce orange juice
½ ounce lemon juice
    dash orange-flower water or orange bitters
2 teaspoons grenadine

Shake ingredients with cracked ice and strain over rocks into prechilled, old-fashioned glass. Add orange slice for garnish. Named for Mexico's largest lake.

# SANGARIA

Not to be confused with Sangría, the wine punch (q.v.).
1 jigger tequila
½ ounce lime juice
4 dashes Tabasco sauce

Combine ingredients with no ice. Down. I have done this one while listening to the Mariachis in a bar at Guadalajara. If the tequila doesn't get you, the Tabasco will!


# BLOODY MARIA

This drink substitutes tequila for the vodka in a bloody mary. Good luck!


# TEQUILA GUAYABA

1 jigger tequila
½ ounce canned guava nectar (S & W puts out an American brand)
½ ounce orange juice
½ ounce lime juice

Shake ingredients with cracked ice and pour over ice cubes into pre-chilled, old-fashioned glass. Garnish with slice of orange.

# TOVARISCH — Vodka, Slivovitz, Akvavit, *et al.*

Few liquors have the wide range of uses as vodka. While the original vodka from the Russia of the Czars may have been distilled from potato mash, modern vodkas make use of a variety of grains such as corn, wheat or rye. Each distiller has his own secret for creating a smooth, clear, tasteless vodka, yet there are nuances of flavor among American vodkas which are easily spotted if you sip a bit from several varieties. If you try Russian vodka, the difference is astounding! It will spoil you for the American brands, just as Polish vodka, which was first served to me by one of my colleagues on the University of Alabama in Birmingham faculty, Dr. Robert Van Sword, a native Pole.

In fine restaurants, and especially in those Russian restaurants such as the Russian Bear in New York City, they will serve vodka ice cold. The first time I had it served this way was in a Russian restaurant in, of all places, Madrid, Spain! The bottle of vodka was frozen in a block of ice. Since the alcohol in vodka prevents it from freezing, this is a different way to serve it. Personally, I keep a bottle of Russian vodka in my freezer for those times when a smooth apèrtif is called for. It sends a delightful message of warmth and good comradeship throughout your being. Thus, Tovarisch!

While vodka is distilled at proofs of 190 or above, it is usually bottled at 80 or 100 proof, and that is what the commonly-found vodkas in America are sold at: Schmirnoff's, Wolfschmitt's, Taaka, etc. Vodka has replaced gin in the martini and gibson, with tonic and in the collins drinks. It also combines a "punch" when mixed with fruit juices of various kinds. Here are a few of the more popular vodka cocktails.

## SCREWDRIVER

1 jigger vodka
orange juice

Put ice cubes in a 6-ounce glass, add vodka, and fill glass with orange juice. Stir. A *Harvey Wallbanger* is easily made from the screwdriver by floating ½ jigger of Galliano liqueur on top.

## BLOODY MARY

A modern classic, the bloody mary is many things to many people, but it is probably most popular as a "bit of the hair" the morning after. Here is a recipe for a half-gallon of the drink to be served to your guests at brunch.

    1 46-ounce can (about 5¾ cups) tomato juice
    2 cups vodka
    2 tablespoons freshly-squeezed lemon juice
    1 teaspoon Worcestershire sauce
    1 tablespoon prepared horseradish
    several drops Tabasco sauce (to suit taste)
    1 teaspoon salt

Combine ingredients in a large pitcher the night before you are going to serve your bloody marys. After twelve hours, pour mixture over ice into highball glasses and garnish with long strips of celery as stirring rods.

## BLOODY MARY JANE

This one is for organic health freaks. Be careful just which herbs you use; some have been declared illegal by the authorities!

    1 quart tomato juice
    1 pint vodka
    8 tablespoons lemon juice
    8 tablespoons organic herbs (to suit your taste)
    1 teaspoon salt
    several dashes Tabasco sauce

Chill overnight. Shake well before serving in highball glasses. Happy flying!

## SNAP-E-TOM BLOODY MARY

There are many bottled and packaged "mixes" for bloody marys, but if you are in a hurry and want a good blend, I think this is one of the best. "Snap-e-tom" is a tomato cocktail made from tomato paste, hot pepper, onion, salt and water. It is readily available in most grocery stores, and comes in "6-packs" of 6-ounce cans or larger.

    1 6-ounce can Snap-e-tom
    2 jiggers vodka
    dash salt
    1 tablespoon lemon juice
    1 dash Worcestershire sauce

Shake well before serving and chill.

## RED ROOSTER

    1 quart cranberry juice
    1 pint vodka
    1 can frozen orange juice

Chill ingredients and combine with cracked ice in blender. Serve as a daiquiri in a champagne glass.

# RUSSIAN WITCH

1 jigger vodka
apple juice
½ lime, freshly-squeezed

Here's one my wife likes. Should be served very cold with wedge of lime for garnish. As served at the Russian Bear in New York.

Equally fiery liquors which derive from plums are distilled in eastern Europe. They are known as slivovitz or sliwowitz. While some connoisseurs feel that this liquor is unpleasant, when it is aged six years in wood and served ice cold, the 100-proof drink is a welcome change from your usual choice. At the Royal Family Liquor Store on St. Charles Avenue in New Orleans I was able to buy an excellent Jerusalem Sliwowitz.

The national drink of the Scandanavians is undoubtedly akvavit or aquavit. You find this served in Iceland, Denmark, Sweden and Norway. Its name derives from the Latin *"aqua vitae"* or water of life. While strong, clear and vodka-like, akvavit has just a hint of caraway seeds, which makes it ideal when served chilled with a plate of cold cuts and cheeses. Although most Danes like to take it neat, here are some variations of the akvavit:

# DANISH MARY

1 jigger akvavit
3 ounces tomato juice
½ lime, freshly squeezed
dash celery salt

Combine ingredients and stir with lots of cracked ice. Pour into 6-ounce tulip glass.

# COPENHAGEN

1 jigger akvavit
½ jigger triple sec
½ jigger lime or lemon juice

Shake well with cracked ice and strain into prechilled cocktail glass.

# Apple Brandy — To Keep the Doctor Away?

While the story of George Washington's having cut down the cherry tree may have been pure fiction, his interest in another fruit was genuine. He wrote to Samuel Laird asking for his recipe for apple brandy. Since 1780 Laird's of Scobeyville, New Jersey has been distilling apple jack, which is the popular name for apple brandy. They put out a blend of 80-proof and a straight brand which has been bottled in bond for at least 7½ years and is 100-proof. The blend has 35% straight apple brandy and 65% grain neutral spirits.

I guess I come by my taste for apple jack naturally. One of my maternal ancestors, Hendrick Hendrickson, wrote his will in 1834 concerning his Monmouth County property. To his son, William, he left the "cider works and casks, stills, fixtures and casks" and all other equipment necessary to the manufacture of cider and apple jack.

New Jersey farmers still take their ripe apples — not overripe — and crush them in a press so that the juice drains through canvas cloths. It is then stored in cool cellars where it slowly ferments. Unfermented apple juice is simple, sweet cider such as you buy in any grocery store. Hard cider, on the other hand, is the fermented product. When hard cider is double-distilled and stored in wooden casks to age, the result is apple jack, or as it was affectionately known during Prohibition, "Jersey Lightning."

Many connoisseurs claim that American apple brandy is inferior to Calvados, a product of Norman France, which is aged in wood for a minimum of ten years before being sold. Calvados is generally lower in alcoholic content than the American apple brandy. Here are the well-known recipes calling for apple jack:

## JACK ROSE

1 part grenadine
8 parts apple brandy, apple jack or Calvados
2 parts freshly-squeezed lemon juice

Shake vigorously with lots of cracked ice and strain into prechilled cocktail glass. Add a twist of lemon. For an added professional touch, moisten the rim of the glass with grenadine and dip in powdered sugar. Shake off excess sugar.

# JERSEY SOUR

1 part simple syrup
2 parts freshly-squeezed lemon juice
8 parts apple brandy

Shake vigorously and serve in prechilled cocktail glass. The difference between the sour and the Jack Rose is the use of simple syrup instead of grenadine.

# BUNNY BONANZA

1 jigger tequila
1 ounce apple brandy
1 teaspoon sugar
½ teaspoon curaçao
½ ounce lemon juice

Shake tequila, apple brandy and other ingredients with cracked ice and strain into prechilled, old-fashioned glass. Add ice to fill glass and garnish with slice of lemon. As developed at the Detroit Playboy Club.

# A Day Without Wine Is Like a Day Without Sunshine

A frozen orange juice concentrate has taken an old Spanish proverb and twisted it around, but when I lived in Andalucía, the expression was "El día sin vino, es como el día sin sol": "A day without wine is like a day without sunshine." Wine has been around for a long time, and during biblical times, just about everyone drank it. Miracles recorded of Jesus Christ include the conversion of water into wine, and the apostle who did so much to create modern Christianity, St. Paul, warned his friend Timothy, "Drink no longer water, but use a little wine for thy stomach's sake." (St. Paul's First Epistle to Timothy, 5:23).

New Orleans has always enjoyed fine wines. Now that wines seem to be going through a rebirth throughout the United States, New Orleans wine cellars are more well-stocked than ever. It is not my intention here to discuss the various types of wines. You can best refer to Thomas Mario, the periodical Vintage, and particularly the Private Guide to Food & Wine, begun by Robert Lawrence Balzer in 1970 and continuing in a series.

The term "room temperature" often puzzles wine drinkers. Just what does it mean? Well, recall that room temperature goes back to medieval times, when a castle without modern heating had a "room temperature" of between 65 and 72 degrees Fahrenheit. Thus, you are advised to chill red wines to keep them below 72°. I can recall several years ago being offered red wine which had been chilled in the refrigerator. It was delicious! Some white wines scintillate with taste when well chilled, but become quite ordinary when they are served warm.

One of the most interesting New Orleans drinks from the colonial period to the present day is Sangría, a wine punch made with fruit, sugar, and lots of ice. Although there are as many variations of this Spanish classic as there are of the chilled vegetable soup known as gazpacho, the basic ingredients are red wine — usually the Spanish Riojas such as Marqués de Riscal or the Valdapeñas wines of central Spain — fresh fruits, sugar and water. Thomas Mario's Sangría recipe calls for a fifth of red wine, cognac, triple sec, lemons, orange, peach, maraschino, and club soda.

Since I frequently serve my guests Sangría from my own special recipe, I include it herewith, with apologies to my Spanish friends for taking such liberties with their classic cooler. When I taught my brother Donald this formula, he took it back with him to Florida State University and introduced it to his fraternity friends. This variation promptly caught on and brought more than one headache to the student body.

# HOLMES SANGRIA

I mix this in a five gallon drum which my uncle painted inside and outside for exactly this purpose. I combine a fifth of vodka with three fifths of dry, red wine. If I can't obtain Spanish Rioja, I find that Italian Swiss Colony or Almadén Burgundy does just as well. Add two cups of sugar and stir until dissolved. Use a wooden spoon for this. Add two cups of freshly-squeezed orange juice, and one cup of fresh lime juice. Add two jiggers maraschino liqueur or add the contents of a jar of maraschino cherries. Slice a half-dozen red delicious apples and remove cores. Add slices to mixture. Cut up a half-dozen oranges and add the slices. Allow this mixture to marinate for a minimum of four hours.

Before serving, put a block of ice in the bottom of a punch bowl, and another block of ice in the mixture. If you don't have a block frozen, ice cubes will do. Add just before the guests are ready to be served. The very last thing to be added is a six-pack of 10-ounce bottles of 7-Up. If mixture is too sweet, add some more lime juice. Lemon juice may be substituted if you do not care for limes. Ladle cold mixture with some of the fruit over an ice cube in punch cups. Warning: this drink, as with other fruit-and-vodka combinations, is deceptive. You don't realize it until you stand up after an evening of these and try to walk a straight line. Definitely not to be combined with driving!

For those who want to try this recipe for a single glass, I make the following mixture:

1 jigger vodka
1 jigger dry, red wine
½ jigger lime or lemon juice
Add ice cubes to a tall, 14-ounce glass, and fill with 7-Up.

As the Catholic princes of Spain used to cry as they launched their attacks against the Moorish castles, *"Santiago y a ellos!"* (St. James and go get 'em!)

# Beer — Man's Oldest and Best Friend

The Kingston Trio popularized an old drinking song a few years ago, in which they harmonized, "Here's to the man who drinks dark ale and goes to bed quite mellow!" James Boswell wrote in 1786, "Come, my lad, and drink some beer." But my favorite quote is by Martha Forbes, who on celebrating her 103rd birthday in 1965, claimed, "Oh, I love my beer. It keeps me from aching!"

Beer is at least 5,000 years old, and may well have been the first alcoholic beverage produced by man. Indeed, the word "booze" comes from the Egyptian malt beverage, "boozah." William Iversen tells of one feast in ancient Memphis where the faithful offered 900 jugs of beer to the god Ptah. Subsequently, revelers polished off a half-million jugs of the brew!

Stanley Baron, who wrote a history of beer and ale in the United States, claims that beer has been a part of man's diet in all known civilizations, a fact which is reinforced by findings of anthropologists. In America, where annual consumption has reached an average of 17 gallons, beer has been an important food since before the Pilgrims landed at Plymouth Rock or Cape Cod. One diarist of the *Mayflower* explained why the ship did not proceed to its destination of Virginia in 1620: "For we could not now take time for further search or consideration, our victuals being much spent, especially our beer."

In early Africa the people fermented their millet beers with milkweed. From the fiords of Scandinavia, the Vikings brought to a thirsty world a beverage called *biorr*. Anglo-Saxon tribes from Germany to England modified the word to the present, "beer." Although it is a popular legend that beer making in the United States dates from the 1848 period when large numbers of German liberals fled political persecution in their homeland and came to the traditional beer centers of the United States in Milwaukee and St. Louis, actually beer had been brewed at least a century before.

An 1899 Schlitz advertisement which appeared in *Harper's Weekly* warned against drinking "green beer", the poorly fermented brew that makes you bilious and gives you sick headaches. At that time Schlitz stored its beers in refrigerating rooms for months before leaving the brewery. Four million cubic feet of air in these rooms was kept at a temperature of 34 degrees. Schlitz in that year produced some 265,000 barrels.

Although New Orleans once boasted a large number of breweries, today there are only three. The most famous — "A New Orleans Tradition" — is undoubtedly Jax (alias Fabacher, which is the family name of the brewers), produced by the Jackson Brewing Company since 1890. The brewery is in the French Quarter, on Decatur Street, opposite Jackson Square. Tours are provided. The old Southern tradition is claimed for another New Orleans beer, Dixie, whose low-key advertising seems to emphasize the leisurely process of brewing which makes Dixie a favorite with many. Falstaff also maintains a brewery on Gravier and a canning plant on Earhart Boulevard.

Visitors to New Orleans are advised that beer is served in cans of two sizes, according to the ranking of the beer. Thus, top-line brands such as Budweiser, Schlitz and Miller's come in 10-ounce cans. Both are supposed to sell at the same price.

# Coffe and Anti-freeze

Among the more distinctive "drinks" of New Orleans, we should not forget the coffee. Louisiana coffee is distinctive because of its roast. Coffees such as Community Club are dark roasted, which gives a strong flavor to the coffee, which is ideally made in special drip pots available throughout the French Quarter. Some coffee, including Luzianne, contains chicory. This valuable herb, which early settlers resented because of its hardy nature — they called it blue-flowered lettuce — was mixed with coffee during the Napoleonic blockades when straight coffee became too expensive. Chicory (*Chichorium intybus* L.) has been found to stimulate the flow of digestive juices and is an excellent compliment to the coffee bean. French Market Coffee sold at the familiar coffee house of that name on Decatur Street opposite Jackson Square, should be taken home so that you can brew your own. Even the rare aroma is enough to bring back fond memories of days and nights in New Orleans!

If you want to serve New Orleans coffee frontier style try

## OLD STYLE BOILED COFFEE

1 cup coarsely-ground coffee
3 quarts cold water (6 pints or 12 8-ounce cups)
2 dashes salt
2 eggshells, well crushed into tiny pieces

Combine coffee, water and salt in an old-fashioned, covered pot and cook slowly until it boils. Boil about 3 minutes, or until mixture rises to pot cover. Remove from heat. Add eggshells. Keep hot until ready to serve. Pour through strainer into 12-15 cups.

New Orleans has a Latin tradition in many aspects of its culture, and this is particularly true in its coffee. Early Spanish settlers wanted their coffee, "black as night, strong as love, and hot as hell." Few places in the country serve as many demi-tasse cups of the dark coffee as does Louisiana. If straight, black coffee is not for you, however, there are variations which are popularly served in the fine restaurants of New Orleans. Here are a few:

## CAPPUCCINO

6 ounces brandy
6 teaspoons ground sweet chocolate
1½ teaspoons instant coffee
6 teaspoons sugar
1 quart hot milk

This recipe serves six. For each mug or glass, combine the coffee, chocolate and sugar. Pour hot milk to within an inch of the rim. Top with an ounce of brandy as you serve.

# CAFE BRULOT

Make like Café Diable, but add a vanilla bean and a stick of cinnamon. By rubbing the sugar cubes with the citrus first, you will have additional flavor nuance.

# CAFE DIABLE

1 cup cognac
1 slice orange
1 slice lemon
2 large sugar cubes
2 whole cloves
1 cup coffee

In a silver bowl warm cognac, sugar, cloves and fruit. With a ladle, dip cognac and light as you lower into bowl. Gradually add coffee into the mixture. Repeat process until the coffee is all added and the flame dies out. Serve in demi-tasse coffee cups.

# CAFE ROYALE

6 coffee measures (12 level tablespoons) French-roast coffee
8 ounces water

Brew coffee in your usual way, thus making double-strength, after-dinner coffee. Pour into 6 demi-tasse cups. Place a sugar cube on tablespoon and fill with cognac. Holding it over the coffee to warm the cognac, ignite the mixture. When flame dies out, stir into coffee. Repeat with other cups (this recipe is for six). You can substitute rum, apple brandy, etc., for the cognac. This is a very popular after-dinner treat in New Orleans.

# IRISH COFFEE

According to one Irish whiskey distiller, Irish coffee was introduced to the American market by visitors to Shannon Airport near Dublin, who sampled the Irish specialty and brought back a taste for the drink.

1 jigger Irish whiskey
1 teaspoon sugar
  hot, freshly-brewed coffee
1 tablespoon Irish whiskey
  whipped cream

Pour jigger into 8-ounce stemmed glass. Heat and ignite the whiskey. Add a teaspoon of sugar and fill glass to within an inch or two of the top with coffee. Fill a tablespoon with Irish whiskey. Heat and allow the whiskey flames to run down the sides of the glass. Float whipped cream on top and serve.

A variation on this favorite is Irish Mist Coffee. Heat a stemmed whiskey goblet or mug. Pour in a jigger of Irish Mist liqueur. Fill goblet with about one-half cup strong hot coffee to within an inch of the brim. Stir. Add 3 tablespoons of whipped cream so that it floats on top. Do not stir! The true flavor is derived from absorbing the coffee through the Irish Mist and the coolness of the whipped cream. The Irish have a toast for this one:

"Irish Mist, smooths as the wit of the land,

Coffee, strong as a friendly hand,

Cream, rich as an Irish brogue."

Although not as well-known as its more famous cousin, Irish Tea is also capable of inducing the warm feeling, so needed in the raw, cold New Orleans winters.

## IRISH TEA

1 jigger Irish whiskey
6 ounces hot, freshly-brewed tea (Irish tea is best)
3 whole cloves
3 whole allspice
1 stick cinnamon
1 slice lemon
1 teaspoon bar sugar
2 teaspoons honey

Place all ingredients except lemon slice in a pre-heated mug. Stir well. Add lemon slice. Grate a whole nutmeg over the top and set mug on hot tray for 10 minutes before serving.

Three other drinks designed to keep out the cold are as follows:

## HOT BUTTERED RUM

1 jigger dark Jamaican rum
1 teaspoon sugar or maple syrup
1 teaspoon butter
3 whole cloves
  dash bitters

Add boiling water to above ingredients and serve in a warm mug.

# BLUE BLAZER

This is a production number, for which you need two silver or pewter mugs. In one, dissolve a tablespoon of honey in enough hot water to fill the mug half full. In the other mug, fill half of it with Scotch. Ignite Scotch and carefully pour into the first mug. If you do this carefully, you can pour back and forth from one mug to the other for about five times before the flame dies out. Serve in a heavy, heat-resistant mug with a twist of lemon peel and dusted with nutmeg.

# GLOGG

1 quart cognac
1 pint sherry
1 dozen whole cloves
½ cup sugar
1 stick of cinnamon
½ cup raisins
½ cup blanched almonds

Combine all ingredients except sherry in a silver bowl and ignite cognac. Stir until sugar is dissolved and flame goes out. While still hot, stir in sherry and serve. This can be stored in air-tight bottle in refrigerator, then reheated almost to boiling point before serving.

# Thanks, But I'm on the Wagon

I have nothing against teetotalers; some of my best friends and former wives shunned "demon rum" as destructive. I do not, however, surrender my basic right to down whatever libation I may prefer, while maintaining their right to drink their own way. To each his own! Here are some drinks that even the W.C.T.U. would not be ashamed to be seen drinking. For your non-alcohol-drinking friends, the "fake cocktails" might save a good deal of unnecessary explaining and see to it that they have as good a time at your party as those who want harder stuff.

## SOUTHERN BEAUTY

1 egg white
½ large lime, freshly squeezed
2 dashes angostura bitters

Shake vigorously with crushed ice.

## PUSSYFOOT

1 part lemon juice
3 parts orange juice
1 teaspoon grenadine
1 egg yolk

Shake thoroughly with cracked ice.

## PROHIBITION HIGHBALL

2 jiggers grape juice
1 lemon, freshly squeezed
½ lime, freshly squeezed
1 jigger raspberry syrup

Mix in tall glass. Add ice cubes and ginger ale. Garnish with slice of lime or mint leaf.

## ANGOSTURA FIZZ

1 pony angostura bitters
1 teaspoon grenadine
½ lime, freshly squeezed
1 tablespoon heavy cream
1 egg white

Combine ingredients with cracked ice and shake vigorously. Pour in goblet and fill with siphon or club soda. Garnish with grated lemon rind and a wedge of fresh pineapple.

# CARDINAL PUNCH

1 quart cranberry juice
1 pint orange juice
2 lemons, freshly squeezed
4 quarts ginger ale

Combine fruit juices with ice and chill. Pour into punch bowl over block of ice and add ginger ale. When serving in punch glasses, garnish with mint sprig.

# SHIRLEY TEMPLE

1 jigger grenadine syrup

Fill high-ball glass with ginger ale and ice. Pierce a cherry and orange slice with toothpick. Serve with tall straw.

# ROSY SOUR

2 cups chilled strong tea
2 cups cranberry juice
1 jigger fresh lemon juice
1 egg white

Whip egg into frothy white and add to mixture. Serve in a whiskey sour glass with slice of orange and cherry.

# SORTA BLOODY MARY

1 6-ounce can of Snap-e-Tom tomato cocktail
dash Worcestershire sauce
dash lemon juice
Tabasco to taste

Chill and serve as a Bloody Mary with celery stick as stirrer.

# PILE DRIVER

4 ounces fresh chilled orange juice (or frozen, if you will)
4 ounces chilled quinine water

Serve over ice cubes in high-ball glass.

# WET MARTEENIE

Instead of the usual martini variations, add a dash of bitters to a glass of chilled club soda. Serve with twist of lemon.

# OLD MAID

4 ounces cola drink
4 ounces lemon-lime drink

Serve over ice cubes and garnish with orange slice and cherry.

INTERIOR OF THE OLD ABSINTHE HOUSE BAR,
CONTI AND BOURBON STREETS
from *Roosevelt Review October, 1938*

— Courtesy of Tulane University

## New Orleans Bars

Many tourists who come to New Orleans for the first time can hardly wait until they stroll down Bourbon Street to see what they suppose is the center of night life in New Orleans. Actually, Bourbon Street has never been the *only* center of night life in the Crescent City. Back in the days of the Spanish Dons, there were only a couple of taverns located there, most of them being situated on Levee Street near the river (present-day Decatur). During the hey-day of the jazz era, the cribs, and the off-color bars, the center was on the edge of the French quarter, along Rampart. Still, some famous bars were located inside the French Quarter.

Of all the New Orleans bars down through the years, two stand out as being preeminent: the Sazerac House and the Old Absinthe House.

## Sazerac House

When Aaron Bird opened the Sazerac Coffee House at 13 Exchange Place in the French Quarter during 1852, he served a fiery distillation known as Sazerac Brandy, after the French firm of Sazerac-de-Forges. It was an immediate success! By 1872 another Sazerac House was opened on Royal Street around the corner from the original Exchange Place coffee house. The Sazerac House boasted a bar some 125 feet long, and the management employed eighteen bartenders to care for the thirst of its many patrons.

EXTERIOR OF THE OLD ABSINTHE HOUSE BAR
— Courtesy of Tulane University, Louisiana Collection

## Old Absinthe House

A must-see tourist attraction, the present "Old Absinthe House" is located at 240 Bourbon Street, on the corner with Bienville. The building was erected soon after Pedro Font and Francisco Juncadella purchased the desirable corner lot from Marie Car on March 23, 1806. At that time it was not a bar; it housed an importer's business. Font and Juncadella were Catalans from Barcelona, and they directed a prosperous trade between New Orleans and their native land. In 1806 the firm built a combination home, and commission business house. The structure remained in the same family for many years, but under various guises — a shoe shop in 1838; a grocery in 1861; a coffee house. By 1870, however, when Cayetano Ferrer came from Barcelona to New Orleans and became the chief mixologist, the "coffee house" was converted into the "Absinthe Room." ,

He installed an elaborate marble fountain, the faucet of which was adjusted to drip a drop at a time. The fountain was filled with absinthe and a glass with ice was placed under the tap. Drip, drip, drip! Voilá, the Absinthe Frappé! By 1890 the house had earned the distinctive title, "The Old Absinthe House."

In time, the absinthe was joined by the Sazerac cocktail. Owen Brennan, known as the "dean of the Old Absinthe House" (and as father of the founder of Brennan's Restaurant), was given credit for changing the recipe for the Sazerac by using bourbon rather than rye.

One of the specialties of the Old Absinthe House today is the "Pirate's Dream," a blend of four kinds of rum served over a bed of crushed mint leaves, passion fruit syrup, ice and fruit garnishes, all of which is served in a huge 28-ounce glass.

## Casa De Los Marinos

In its hey-day, the Casa de los Marinos was one of the most atmospheric spots in New Orleans. Located on Decatur Street opposite the Jackson Brewing Company, it was the tavern embodiment of the "Peter Principle." That is, its success led it to expand and alter until it reached the level of its incompetence. Picture a typically-Latin juke box, with records from Cuba, Mexico, and the rest of Latin America, beer at a quarter a can, mixed drinks for 50 cents, a clientele of sailors enjoying shore leave after months at sea at the far corners of the earth, several sets of conga and bongo drums, maracas, raspas, all the percussion instruments popular among Latin Americans. As the juke box blared a favorite, customers borrowed the percussion instruments and played along, improvising in the best New Orleans jazz tradition. For a few dollars you could spend a fine evening, meet some fascinating people, do your soul some good, and have some great memories. Soon, the word got around and Tulane students "discovered" the Casa. So did a rather undesirable clientele. Beer went up, and mixed drinks joined. Prosperity expanded the original bar into three adjoining buildings, each of which had its own bar and entertainment. Did success spoil the Casa? You bet! Violations of New Orleans regulations, particularly against serving minors, brought police surveillance. Old customers fell away, and the new breed was insensitive to the problems. Today the Casa de los Marinos is no more than a memory, but it sure was fun in its day! Wasn't it, Linda?

## Cosimo's Bar

Another of the "atmosphere" places, Cosimo's is at 1201 Burgundy, quite a walk from Canal Street, because it is at the other end of the French Quarter. The walk is worth it. For more than a decade this has been a place for good friends, good drinks, reasonable prices, and some of the most original, impromptu music still available in New Orleans. If they haven't changed the rules, you could go to Cosimo's with your particular instrument and join the jam session. I have not enjoyed this kind of place anywhere else in New Orleans, although the banjos, beer and hand-clapping at Your Father's Mustache comes close. This is like the Latin bars in Mexico or Spain, where anyone who gets the spirit, can strum a few Flamenco cords on his guitar and sing a plaintiff *saeta,* or a famous Mexican movie star will be asked to sing for the patrons. This happened once in 1954 when I was having a meal at Las Cazuelas in Mexico City. The mariachi rose by his table and obliged his grateful audience, after which he returned to his *caldo de médula.* An evening at Cosimo's should be a real treat!

## Playboy Club

Although the Playboy Club is usually "off-limits" to non-key-members, the New Orleans club is sometimes permissive about letting "strangers" enjoy the fine drinks and entertainment. When they opened their doors to the public in 1972, the crowds filled the club and made things a bit uncomfortable for the key-holding members. The major attraction of a Playboy Club varies according to the night club artists which are currently featured, but one thing which is regular is the quality of the drinks served at the Playboy bar. They are reasonable, well-mixed, and attractively served.

## Top of the Mart

Since the construction of the International Trade Mart with its revolving lounge on the 33rd floor, hundreds of visitors to New Orleans have walked down Canal Street toward the Mississippi River to Number 2. Elevators speed you into the skies from 10 A.M. to 2 A.M. except on weekends. Saturday's hours are 11 A.M. to 3 A.M. Sundays the lounge is open from 4 P.M. til midnight. Whether you are an old-timer or a newcomer to New Orleans, this is a "must." Enjoying a well-mixed drink, you sit still as the lounge rotates very slowly (it takes about an hour to make a complete revolution) and the beauty of the Crescent City and its magnificent river unfolds before your eyes. During Carnival when flambeaux parades through the Quarter plunge into thousands of visitors, shouting "Throw me a doubloon," the view is superb. A Pirate's Gold drink served at that time, comes complete with its doubloon (orange juice and rum).

## Roosevelt Hotel

No one who has traveled through the southern states at night can forget the radio broadcasts emanating from the Blue Room of the Roosevelt Hotel. The hotel has more than that one bar, however, and devotees of New Orleans night life can enjoy their favorite drinks in the Fairmont, Rendezvous, and Sazerac Bars. At the Blue Room there is a cover charge because there is always a headliner show, beginning at 9 and 11:30 P.M., except for Sundays. The Fairmont Court also charges a cover charge to its patrons; it is open Tuesdays through Sundays from 10 P.M. to 2 A.M.

## The Economy Hall

Those travelers who are on a budget should welcome this attractive bar in the Royal Sonesta Hotel (300 Bourbon Street). The entertainment charge as of this writing was $1.75, but there is no minimum. Drinks are a modest $1.60. There is always a good New Orleans jazz group here. For those desiring a slightly different ambiance, there is the Mystic Den in the same hotel.

## Victorian Lounge

The Holiday Inn at 124 Royal Street has a lounge on the 10th floor, which is open from Monday through Saturday, 9 P.M. til 1 A.M. There is no cover, no minimum.

## Pete Fountain's French Quarter Inn

Located at 231 Bourbon Street, the mellifluous sounds of Pete Fountain's clarinet have made this one of the top night spots in New Orleans. Open Tuesday-Saturday from 4 P.M., Pete himself appears in shows beginning at 9:15. Always crowded, but worth the wait and the rather steep prices. Not recommended during Carnival: it's a madhouse then!

## Le Centime Lounge

Located at the corner of Baronne and Poydras, this underground lounge has no cover, no minimum. It is a comfortable lounge with entertainment from Monday through Saturday beginning at 9 P.M.

## El Cid's Nite Club

Located in the Sheraton-Delta Motor Hotel at 1732 Canal, this lounge has no cover or minimum. During the winter season it is open from 9 P.M. to 2 A.M., and there is good entertainment.

## Sheraton-Charles

This hotel, located on St. Charles just a block away from the French Quarter and Canal, has a Polynesian-type lounge called the Outrigger. The specialty of the house is the Planter's Punch.

## Cafe Lafitte

Once located at 941 Bourbon, alas, this tavern is no more. The specialty of the house used to be a dry martini with a lingering taste of absinthe, which they called the Obituary. Apparently, the Obituary brought on the death of the establishment . . .

## Pontalba's Taverne

Located at 60 St. Peter Street, on the corner with Chartres, there is a legend that this moresque structure was once the famous tavern called "Le Veau-qui-Tête" or "Suckling Calf." Not so! The real "Veau-qui-Tête" was located at the old Rue de la Levée #58 (present-day Decatur Street, #919). In the early days R. Ravel kept there a tavern, inn, public baths, and the finest stock of wines and liquor in the city.

## Napoleon House

Down through the years the legend has persisted that a group of Napoleon's former soldiers plotted here to spirit their former commander away from St. Helena and set him up in the home of Nicholas Girod, mayor of New Orleans, who owned this house. Taverns and bars have come and gone in the quarter, all of them called "Napoleon House." Charming legend, but bare of fact!

## Commander's Palace

In the Garden District on the corner of Washington and Coliseum there is an outstanding restaurant with a charming bar, dating to the year 1880 (which is why they call it "The 1880 Bar"). This is one of the few vestiges of the 19th century which Commander's has preserved. On Easter Sunday in 1947 a disastrous fire destroyed most of the restaurant, and only the pleas of the faithful many who had tippled at the old bar, persuaded the builders to restore as much of the original as possible. Shirt-sleeved bartenders with their garters prepare excellent drinks so that waiting for a table at the restaurant is really one of the pleasant interludes of dining there.

## Your Father's Mustache

Get a kick out of old banjo playing, draft beer, and good, clean fun? This night club at 426 Bourbon is suggested for a rousing good time and not a little bit of nostalgia.

The list of good New Orleans night life, entertainment, taverns, bars, and strip joints could occupy a book in itself. Most New Orleans motels and hotels provide free copies of a "See New Orleans" free souvenir guide," which is published twice a month. The "After Dark" section contains much current information on who is appearing at what club, together with addresses. It is difficult to realize that in 1769 Governor Alexander O'Reilly permitted only six taverns to operate in all of New Orleans. In 1973 there are over 500! The following list of night clubs with addresses and phone numbers is based on information available in January, 1973:

# New Orleans nights clubs as of January, 1973:

| | | |
|---|---|---|
| AL HIRT NIGHT CLUB | 501 Bourbon | 525-6167 |
| BACKSTAGE 500 | 808 St. Louis | 523-0031 |
| BAYOU ROOM | 321 Bourbon | 523-0905 |
| BISTRO CLUB & LOUNGE | 4061 Tulane Ave. | 482-9377 |
| BLUE ROOM | University Place | 524-8885 |
| (Fairmont Roosevelt Hotel) | | |
| BREAUX'S BAR | 537 Ave. A, Marrero | 347-8120 |
| BRENT'S FRANKIE CLUB | 2201 David Dr., Metairie | 885-7764 |
| CABARET THEATRE | | |
| (Old Absinthe Bar) | 400 Bourbon | 525-1226 |
| CELLAR | 1100 Stephens, Gretna | 361-9681 |
| CHO CHO SAN LOUNGE | 201 Royal | 581-9513 |
| CIRO'S CHATEAU FLAMENCO | 730 St. Peter | 525-3233 |
| CISSY'S CAMEO LOUNGE | 1429 St. Charles Ave. | 523-9680 |
| CLUB MY-O-MY | 940 Conti | 523-1653 |
| CLUB PENCHEROU'S | | |
| MOTOR LODGE | 1734 Carondelet | 523-8404 |
| COSIMO'S BAR | 1201 Burgundy | 523-9818 |
| CROW'S NEST | 2105 Hancock, Gretna | 361-9819 |
| DELLA'S PLACE | 4240 Clio | 822-9910 |
| DIRECTOIRE | 825 Toulouse | 529-2945 |
| DIXIE'S BAR | 540 Burgundy | 523-0150 |
| DOROTHY'S MEDALLION | 3232 Orleans Ave. | 482-9239 |
| DOWNS LOUNGE | 3112 Downs Blvd., Metairie | 887-9928 |
| ECONOMY HALL | | |
| (Royal Sonesta Hotel) | 300 Bourbon | 529-3711 |
| 800 CLUB | 800 Bourbon | 523-0097 |
| EIGHT-O-NINE CLUB | 500 Bourbon | 522-6094 |
| EL SOMBRERO | 231 Bourbon | 523-0250 |
| FAMOUS DOOR BAR | 339 Bourbon | 523-9973 |
| FIVE HUNDRED CLUB | 441 Bourbon | 525-7269 |
| FUN HOUSE | 2104 Magazine | 523-9880 |
| GAY TIMES | 405 Bourbon | 581-2314 |
| GUNGA DEN | 325 Bourbon | 523-8391 |
| HOTSY TOTSY | 232 Bourbon | 523-8703 |
| HUKI-LAU | 3701 Hessmer, Metairie | 888-5816 |
| IVANHOE PIANO BAR | 601 Bourbon | 523-0930 |
| JEFFERSON-ORLEANS | 2536 Edenborn, Metairie | 885-4422 |
| KIVA LOUNGE | 8332 Chef Menteur Hwy. | 242-9723 |
| L. & S. LOUNGE | 1107 St. Anthony | 943-1068 |
| LA DONNA VILLA LOUNGE | 1496 4th, Westwego | 341-8231 |
| LIVING ROOM | 327 Bourbon | 523-8793 |
| MANDALAY ROOM | 435 Newton | 361-9298 |
| MICHELI'S | 5163 Gen. de Gaulle Dr. | 394-9764 |
| MOULIN ROUGE | 5514 4th, Marrero | 347-8156 |
| MY-O-MY CLUB | 940 Conti | 523-1653 |
| NASHVILLE LOUISIANA | | |
| CLUB | 6979 N. Peters, Arabi | 279-9552 |
| NEW GARDEN CLUB | 209 Monroe, Gretna | 361-9355 |
| NEW 77 CLUB | 808 N. Claiborne | 581-9689 |
| NIGHT CAP LOUNGE | 1700 Louisiana Ave. | 899-9177 |
| OLD ABSINTHE BAR | 400 Bourbon | 523-8730 |
| OLD ABSINTHE HOUSE | 240 Bourbon | 523-8833 |
| PADDOCK BAR & LOUNGE | 309 Bourbon | 523-9648 |
| PAPA JOE'S RINGSIDE | | |
| LOUNGE | 423 Bourbon | 523-8476 |
| PARKER'S PLAYBOY CLUB | 3725 Magazine | 895-9278 |
| PAT O'BRIEN'S | 718 St. Peter | 525-4823 |
| PETE FOUNTAIN FRENCH | | |
| QUARTER INN | 231 Bourbon | 523-4374 |

| | | |
|---|---|---|
| PETE'S 800 CLUB | 800 Bourbon | 525-3862 |
| PLACE ACROSS THE STREET | 3120 Severn, Metairie | 889-0223 |
| PLAYBOY CLUB | 727 Iberville | 523-5001 |
| QUARTER NOTE LOUNGE | 3721 Hessmer, Metairie | 889-0531 |
| RUSS RUSSELL'S STAGECOACH INN | 2125 U.S. 90, Avondale | 776-8951 |
| SAFARI LOUNGE | 706 Iberville | 523-9709 |
| SILVER DOLLAR LOUNGE | 129 Sala, Westwego | 347-8155 |
| SOUL BROTHERS CLUB | 3700 S. Claiborne | 895-9329 |
| TAIL OF THE COCK | 3006 Cleary, Metairie | 885-6091 |
| TOUCHE OF ROYAL ORLEANS | 621 St. Louis | 529-5333 |
| UNCLE SAM'S | 829 St. Charles Ave. | 523-0741 |
| WHITEY'S DEVIL'S DEN | 2121 Banks | 523-9174 |
| YOUR FATHER'S MUSTACHE | 426 Bourbon | 523-1810 |
| YVONNE'S LIVING ROOM | 1300 St. Bernard Ave. | 947-9507 |

## Pat O'Brien's

This New Orleans "institution" deserves a special section, for no one who enjoys the night life of New Orleans can fail to pay a visit to the bar which has the slogan, "Have Fun!" Also, this is the home of the legendary "Hurricane."

Located at 718 St. Peter Street (between Bourbon and Royal), Pat O'Brien's stands on the site of the first Spanish theatre which goes back to 1792. Several bars nestle around the Spanish Patio, and anyone can enjoy this New Orleans institution.

During Carnival (Mardi Gras week), would-be tipplers, are required to purchase $5.00 worth of "doubloons," which "Irish dollars" are sold at the entrance. They are pretty souvenirs of Carnival, even if you don't use them up at one or another of Pat's bars.

The Hurricane is Pat's contribution to good fun. The glass is a distinctive one, reminiscent of the old-fashioned kerosene lantern and is made to order in Mexico. The hurricane is easy to make in your own home, providing you supply yourself with a passion fruit cocktail mix, such as that made by Jero. It comes in red and green. For the hurricane, you need the red.

### HURRICANE

2 ounces Jero Passion Cocktail Mix (red)
2 ounces freshly-squeezed lemon juice
4 ounces dark, amber rum (definitely not the 151-proof ones!)

Shake ingredients with cracked ice and pour into the 24-ounce hurricane glass. Decorate with slice of orange, maraschino cherry, and serve with two long straws.

Since Pat O'Brien's allows you to buy glass and drink together, get a pair of them and take them home so you can make your own and think of how great the Quarter was . . .

## SQUALL

1 ounce green Jero Passion cocktail mix
1 ounce freshly-squeezed lemon juice
2 ounces good light rum

Shake ingredients with cracked ice and pour into a 16-ounce hurricane glass. Garnish with slice of orange, cherry, and serve with straws.

During Carnival, Pat's offers an interesting variety of drinks from the colorful green Shillelagh, the Purple People Eater, and the Cyclone, to more mundane versions of the use of rum, gin, and the colorful cordials. One word of warning: do not be fooled by the "fruit juice" appearance of these colorful libations. My wife did during Carnival a few years ago, and she still recalls with pain the sorrowful after-effects! Get the bartender to share some of his secrets with you if you get there during a lull. During Carnival, everything is done on a mass-production, assembly-line basis, and you will be lucky to get your change in the rush! By all means, do not leave New Orleans without a visit to Pat O'Brien's, or you will have missed a basic part of what is to be done in the Quarter.

# Toasts for the Occasion

Ever noticed how each national culture seems to come up with its own special toast  Here is a basic primer of toasts based on the traditional American, "Here's Luck!" or the British, "Cheers!"

Wen Lie! (Chinese)
A votre santé (French)
Prosit! (German)
Yasas! (Greek)
L'Chaim! (Hebrew)
Ege'sze'ge're! (Hungarian)
Slainte! (Irish)
Alla Salute! (Italian)
Kanpai! (Japanese)
Na Zdrowie! (Polish)
Za vashe zdorovye! (Russian)
Salud! (Spanish)
Skal! (Swedish)

I can recall a visit to Dublin in 1964 and drinking a toast with an amiable Irish host. I never got the spelling right, but it seems like he was saying, "Shlathern-go-sail-a-goot." Health and happiness is what he meant, and after a few rounds of good Irish whiskey, if you come close, I'm sure your Irish guest will understand what you are trying to say.

Another famous Irish toast is appropriately engraved on some of the Irish coffee cups on sale: "May you be in Heaven a half hour before the devil knows you're dead."

Still another old Irish toast is the following:

"Health and long life to you.
Land without rent to you.
A child every year to you (!).
And may you die in Ireland."

Spanish toasts are as many as there are Spanish-speaking people, but some of the favorite ones are

"Salud, pesetas y amor
y tiempo para gozarlos."
(Health, wealth and love, and time in which to enjoy them).
"Vinos y amores, los viejos son los mejores."
(Wines and friends, the old ones are the best).
"Sin bolsa rellena, ni rubia, ni morena."
(Without a full purse, neither blonde nor brunette).

My friends in Tennessee at Jack Daniel's distillery have some classic folk toasts apropos of the region and the fine liquor they distill:

"May your sons be brave, your daughters marriageable, your wife loving, and your kinfolks rich."

"May you ride an easy-walking horse, sleep 'neath a rain-tight roof, and eat high on the hog every day of the year."

"May you always have red-eye gravy with your ham, hush-puppies with your catfish, and the good sense not to argue with your wife."

Old classic toasts suitable for the man in the rat-race of American business include the following:

"May the most you wish for be the least you get!"

"May the years treat you kindly . . . and your friends follow suit!"

"Here's to prosperity . . . and the wisdom to use it well!"

"May we live to learn well . . . and learn to live well!"

For your good friends, the following toasts should serve:

"Here's to cold nights, warm friends . . . and a good drink to give them!"

"Here's to friendship . . . a story without end!"

"Here's to good whiskey . . . and a good friend to share it with!"

For the romantic of heart, there are always some toasts such as the following:

"May we kiss those we please, and please those we kiss!"

"Here's to the pictures on my desk. May they never meet!"

"Here's to the game they call Ten Toes;
It's played all over town.
The girls all play with ten toes up,
And the boys with ten toes down!"

"Here's to the ladies . . . they need no praise . . . they speak for themselves."

In conclusion, I draw upon the noted pen of Richard B. Sheridan, that 18th century wit, who wrote in his *School for Scandal*:

"Here's to the maiden of bashful fifteen;
Here's to the widow of fifty;
Here's to the flaunting, extravagant queen,
And here's to the housewife that's thrifty.
Let the toast pass —
Drink to the lass;
I'll warrant she'll prove an excuse for the glass."

# More Reading About Booze

Balzer, Robert Lawrence. *Private Guide to Food & Wine.* 1970-date (a continuing series). There are 12 issues to a volume, and Volumes I and II with binder sell for $25.00 each at The Wine Press, Ltd., 682 El Rancho Road, Santa Barbara, Calif. 93108.

Barnard, Charles N. "Cognac, the Happy Accident." *Signature,* October, 1971, pp. 38-43.

Baron, Stanley. *Brewed in America, a History of Beer and Ale in the United States.* Boston: Little, Brown & Co., 1962.

Berry, C. J. J. *First Steps in Winemaking.* Andover, England: Standard Press, 1960.

Bespaloff, Alexis. "All Right, What About California Wines?" *Travel & Leisure,* II, No. 6 (December-January, 1973), 42-45.

————————————. "Frankly, Do You Know How to Order Wine in a Restaurant" *Travel & Leisure,* December-January, 1971-1972.

Calvert Distillers Company (comp. and ed.). *The Calvert Party Encyclopedia.* New York: Calvert Distillers Co., 1960.

Coro, Mason. *In High Spirits.* A series appearing in newspapers around the country, concerned primarily with wine.

Daley, Robert. "How to Bring Bordeaux Back Alive." *Signature,* May, 1971, p. 32-34.

Dart, Henry P. "Cabarets of New Orleans in the French Colonial Period." *Louisiana Historical Quarterly,* XIX, No. 3 (July, 1936), 578-583.

Elson, John T. "Cognac, the Grand Favorite — from Napoleon and Lord Byron to Churchill." *Travel and Leisure,* April-May, 1971, pp. 58-59.

Embury, David A. *The Fine Art of Mixing Drinks.* Garden City, New York: Doubleday, 1949.

Holmes, Jack D. L. (ed.). "O'Reilly's Regulations on Booze, Boarding Houses and Billiards." *Louisiana History,* VI, No. 3 (Summer, 1965), 293-300.

————————————. "Spanish Regulation of Taverns and the Liquor Trade in the Mississippi Valley." *The Spanish in the Mississippi Valley.* Edited by John Francis McDermott. Urbana: University of Illinois Press, 1973.

Gaskill. Gordon. "They're Forever Growing Bubbles." *Signature,* August, 1971, pp. 27-29.

Iversen, William, "Keg O' My Heart." *Playboy,* June, 1965, 143-144, 154, 166-169.

Leake, Dr. Chauncey, and Dr. Milton Silverman. *Alcoholic Beverages in Clinical Medicine.* Cleveland: World Publishing Co., 1966.

Lemkowitz, Florence. "Bacchus is Alive and Well and Living in New York State." *Signature,* June, 1969, pp. 39-40, 72.

Mario, Thomas. "The Case for American Wines." *Playboy,* May, 1966. pp. 104-106, 191-192.

——————————. *Playboy's Host and Bar Book.* Chicago: Playboy Club, 1971.

Massee, William E. "Stocking the Urban Wine Cellar." *Playboy,* February, 1971, pp. 87-90, 184.

Shane, Ted. *Bar Guide.* New York: Fawcett Publications, 1950.

Tritton, S. M. *Tritton's Guide to Better Wine & Beer Making for Beginners.* London: Faber and Faber, 1965.

*Vintage,* a serial publication on wines beginning in 1972.

Waugh, Alec. "Port Wine, a Perfect Reason to Leave the Ladies." *Signature,* January, 1973, pp. 40-42.

Wechsberg, Joseph. "Champagne Country." *Playboy,* August, 1971, pp. 121-122, 156-160.

# INDEX

Absinthe: as morning-after remedy, 19; drinks with, 22-23; frappé, 22; history, 21-22; popularity in New Orleans, 12; suisesse, 22

*Aguardiente de caña*, 53

Alabama: liquor laws, 6; mixed drink known as, 48

Alexander, Brandy, 34

Angostura: bitters, 25; fizz, 74

*Anís:* del Mono, 37; Chinchón, 37

Anisette: popularity in early New Orleans, 12; as a cordial, 37

Anti-freeze, 70-73

Apple Brandy, 64-65

Apple Jack, 64-65

Armagnac, 46

Baily, Francis: enjoys porter in New Orleans, 12; remarks on New Orleans drinking, 12

Baltimore Bracer, 38

Banana: Daiguiri, 36; liqueur, 36; rum frappé, 36

Barbados Planters' Punch, 56

Baroco: cocktail, 56; John, 56

Bars, in New Orleans, 76-85

Base ingredient, 9

Batavian rum, 55

Beer: brewery visits, 5; consumption in early New Orleans, 12; prices in early New Orleans, 12; history of, 68; breweries in New Orleans, 68-69; size of cans in New Orleans, 69

Benedictine, 36, 37

Bienville, Sieur de (Jean Baptiste LeMoyne), 10

Bird, Aaron, 24, 76

Bitters, 24-25

Black Cow, 35

Black Russian, 35

Blackberry Tequila, frozen, 59

Bloody María, 60

Bloody Mary, 61-62

Bloody Mary Jane, 62

Bloody Mary, sorta, 75

Blue Blazer, 73

Blue Room, 80

Booze: origin of word, 68; more reading about, 88-89

Boré, Etienne de, 12

Bourbon, 39

Brainstorm, 37

Brandied pineapple, 48

Brandy: popularity in New Orleans, 11; cost at New Orleans, 11; Alexander, 34; origins, 45-47; ritual, 47; use in brandied pineapple, 48; use in cherry bounce, 32; Spanish brands, 46; Pisco of Peru, 46; Metaxa of Greece, 46-47; California, 47; fruit types, 47; apple, 64-65; Sazerac, 77

Brennan's Restaurant, 19-20

Bronx, 51

Broussard's Restaurant, 38

Budweiser, 69

Bunny Bonanza, 59, 65

B.Y.O.B., 9
Cabildo (City Council), 12
Cacao: Crème de, 35; mit Nuss, 35
Café: Brulot, 71; Diable, 71; Lafitte, 81; Royale, 71
California Driver, 48
Calvados, 64
Canadian Whisky, 40, 44
Cappuccino, 70
Cardinal Punch, 75
Carta Blanca, 5
Casa de los Marinos, 78-79
Cascade Distillers, 39
Cataluña, wines of, 5
Centime Lounge, 81
Cervecería Cuauhtémoc, 5
Chapala, 59
Chartreuse, 35-36
Cherry Bounce, 32
Cherry liqueur, 12
Cider, 12, 64
Cid's Nite Club, 81
Clam juice, 18
Cocktail, origin of, 6-7
Coconut snow mix, 37
Coffee (see also, Café): Lanfray, 23; New Orleans types, 70; with chicory, 70; boiled, 70; Irish, 71-72
Cognac, 45-47
Coinage, American origins, 55
Coleman, Bob and Cathy, 3
Comfort: Collins, 30; Manhattan, 30; Sour, 30
Commander's Palace Restaurant, 82
Copenhagen, 63
Coquetier, 7
Cordials, 33-38
Cosimo's Bar, 79
Craig, Elijah (Rev.), 39
Crème de Menthe, 35
Crème de Moka, 35
Crème de Noyeaux, 35
Crozat, Antoine, 10
Cuarenta y Tres (43), 37
Daiquiri, banana, 36
Damiana, 37
Daniel's, Jack, 39, 41-42, 87
Danish Mary, 63
De la Croix Marron, Chevalier, 45
Delongua, Mr., 13
Demerara rum, 55
Deutsch, Hermann, 31
Dickel, George, 39
Dixie, 69
Drambuie, 40

Dubonnet: cocktail, 52; Tequila, 59
Economy Hall, 80
Embury, David, 41
Eye-openers, 18-20
Fabacher, 68
Falstaff, 69
Ferrer, Cayetano, 78
*Filet*, 53
Fizzes, 27-28
Foggy Day, 51
Font, Pedro, 77
Fountain, Pete (French Quarter Inn), 80
Frappé: Absinthe, 22, 78; crème de menthe, 35; banana rum, 36
Fruit recipes, 31-32, 48
Galicia, wines of, 5
Galliano, 38
Gayoso de Lemos, Manuel, 53
Gibson, 52
Gin: popularity in early New Orleans, 12; drinks made with, 49-52
Glasses: prechilling, 9; sugar frosting, 9, 64; salt frosting, 9; types, 9; absinthe drip glasses, 23
Glogg, 73
Golden Cadillac, 38
Grasshopper, 34
Grog, 53
Guinness, 5
Haiti rum, 55
Hamilton, Alexander, 12
Hammond, Louisiana, 31
Harvey Wallbanger, 38
Hawaiian rum, 55
Hawaiian Snow Job, 37
Heineken's beer, 5
Hendrickson, Hendrick, 64
Herbsaint: New Orleans liquor, 22; New Orleans drink, 22-23; Française, 23
Honolulu Cooler, 29
Hurricane, 84
Il Magnifico, 37
Indians, and liquor, 53-54
Irish: Alexander, 43; Almendra, 44; Coffee, 71-72; Luck, 43; Mist, 40-41; Mist Coffee, 72; Tea, 72; Toasts, 86; Whiskey, 40
Jack Daniel's Whiskey, 39, 41-42, 87
Jack Rose, 64
Jackson Brewing Company, 5, 68-69
Jacquin, Charles, 21-22
Jamaica rum, 54
Jax Beer, 68-69
Jero Passion Cocktail Mix, 55, 84, 85
Jersey Lightning, 64
Jersey Sour, 65
Jump Up and Kiss Me, 38
Juncadella, Francisco, 77

Jung, L. E., and Wolff Company, 25
Kahlúa, 35
Kentucky Whiskey, 39
Kerry Cooler, 43
Knucklehead (Rusty Nail), 42
Kümmel, 35
Ladies' Luck, 34
Lafitte, Jean, 35
Laird, Samuel, 64
Lanfray, Jean, 21
Laws:  governing wines, 11; restrictions on taverns, 10-15
Lemonade, 15
*Limón,* 58
Lind, Jenny, 10
Liqueurs, 33-38, 40-41
Livingston, Robert R., 11
Lóewenbrau, 5
Lotus Club, 22
Magnifico, 11, 37
Maguey, 57
Manhattan, 41
Marc, 45
Margarita, 9, 59
Mario, Thomas, 9, 89
Martinez, 52
Martinez, Raymond J., 52
Martini, 50, 52
Measurements, 8
Méndez, Antonio, 12
Menthe, Crème de, 35
Metaxa, 46-47
Mezcal, 58
Mézières, Athanase de, 12
Milk, 18
Miller's, 69
Mixologist tips, 8-9
Modifying agent, 9
Morales, Juan Buenaventura, 16-17
Moris, Pedro, 15
Morning Glory, 19
Morro, 51
Myers Rum Company, 54
Mystic Den, 80
Napoleon House, 81
Navy Grog Cocktail, 56
New England Rum, 55
New Orleans:  cocktail, 29; Lotus Club, 22
Nichols, Austin, 39
Nine Tumblers Club of St. Andrew, 40
Noyeaux, Crème de, 35
O'Brien's, Pat, 84-85
Ojen Cocktail, 19

Old Absinthe House, 76, 77-78
Old Fashioned, 41
Old Maid, 75
Old Pepper, 19
Olivares, Marcos, 12
Opal, 35
Oracabessa, 36
Ordinaire, Pierre (Dr.), 21
O'Reilly, Alexander (Conde de), 10, 13-15
Orgeat (Orzata), 27
Over-indulgence, 18-20
Parties, preparation for, 9
Pat O'Brien's, 84-85
Peppermint Schnapps, 35
Pernod, 21
Pete Fountain's French Quarter Inn, 80
Peychaud, Antoine Amedie: immigrant to New Orleans, 24; develops Peychaud bitters, 24
Pile Driver, 75
Pink: Gin, 50; Lady, 50; Squirrel, 34
Pirate's Dream, 78
Pisco, 46
Pittman, Philip (Captain), 6, 53-54
Planter's Punch, 55
Playboy Club: Detroit, 59; New Orleans, 26, 79
Polynesian Pick-Me-Up, 19
Pontalba's Taverne, 81
Pousse-Café, 33
Prairie Oyster, 18
Prince Edward, 43
Prohibition Highball, 74
Puerto Rico, rums of, 54
Pulque, 57
Pussyfoot, 74
Quebec, 44
Rainbow, 34
Ramos, Henry, and gin fizz, 27
Ready-mix flavors, 33
Red Baron, 51
Red Rooster, 62
Rioja wines, 10, 12
Robin, C. C., 11
Rob Roy, 42
Roosevelt Hotel, 80
Rosy Sour, 75
Rum: punch, 56; types, 53-55; hot-buttered, 72
Russian Witch, 63
Rusty Nail, 42
Rye Whiskey, 39
St. Patrick, 40
Salt frost, 9
Sangaría, 60

Sangría, 12, 66-67
San Sebastián, 52
Sazerac: Company, 6; House, 24, 76-77; Cocktail, 24-26; Ready-to-Serve
    cocktail mix, 26
Scarlett O'Hara, 29
Schlitz, 68
Scorpion, 34
Scotch: Sling, 43; Solace, 42; Whisky, 39, 40, 73
Screwdriver, 61
Sévigné, Marquise de, 21
Shane, Ted, 18, 33, 89
Sheraton-Charles, 81
Sheridan, Richard B., 87
Sherry, 46, 50
Shirley Temple, 75
Sicilian Gold, 36
Side Car, 48
Siegert, J. G. B. (Dr.), 25
Singapore Sling, 51
Siphon, 27
Slivovitz (Sliwowitz), 63
Sloe Gin: described, 49; Fizz, 28
Smith, Archie R., Jr. (Mrs.), 31
Snap-E-Tom Bloody Mary, 62
Solis, Joseph, 12
Sorta Bloody Mary, 75
Sour Mash, 39
Southern Beauty, 74
Southern Comfort, 29-30
Spanish toasts, 86
Squall, 85
Stinger, 47
Strawberries Amarettini, 31
Strawberry White Port, 32
Tafia, 11, 13, 53
Tariffs on liquor imports to Louisiana, 16-17
Taverns: French laws on, 10; Spanish laws on, 10-15; cost of licenses for,
    14-16; food served in, 14; license fees from used for charity hospital, 15
Teetotalers, drinks for, 74-75
Tennessee: Squires, 42; Whiskey, 39
Tequila: Production of, 57-58; Dubonnet, 59; Guayaba, 60
Tía María, 35
Tiger Tail, 23
Toasts, 86-87
Tomato Juice, 18
Top of the Mart, 79-80
Tuaca, 37
Turtle, 56
Ulloa, Antonio de, 10
Union Jack, 33
Valdapeñas wines, 5, 12
Vaudreuil, Marquise de (Pierre Rigaut), 10

Vermouth, 41, 50
Vernon, Admiral, 53
Victorian Lounge, 80
Virgin Islands rum, 54
Vodka:  production of, 61; drinks using, 61-63
Wallbanger, Harvey, 38
Washington, George, 64
Water, 6
Wet Marteenie, 75
Wheelock, Eleazer, 53
Whiskey:  popularity in New Orleans, 11-12; nicknames for, 12; cost, 12; spelling of, 39; different types of, 39-40; popularity of American, in Europe, 39; Sour, 42
Wild Turkey, 39
Wine, 5, 66
Xerez, 46
Yellow Bird, 38
Your Father's Mustache, 82
Zombie, 55